331.6
Hea

11567

331.6
Hea

11567

Heaps, Willard

Wandering workers

DONATED
TO
WESTMONT HIGH SCHOOL LIBRARY
BY
MATTHEW SMITH
Class of 1968
WHO DIED FOR HIS COUNTRY IN VIETNAM
1969

Wandering Workers

Other Books by Willard A. Heaps

The Story of Ellis Island
Riots, U.S.A. 1765–1965
The Wall of Shame
The Bravest Teenage Yanks

Wandering Workers

by Willard A. Heaps

The Story of American Migrant
Farm Workers and Their Problems

CROWN PUBLISHERS, INC., NEW YORK

The quotation on page 11 is reprinted with the permission of The Macmillan Company from *The Other America* by Michael Harrington, copyrighted by Michael Harrington, 1962.

Acknowledgment is made for the valuable assistance given the author by federal and state government personnel, United States and state senators and congressmen, and organization officials in offering information and supplying publications essential to the writing of this book.

Library of Congress
Catalog Card Number: 68–9061
Printed in the United States of America
Published simultaneously in Canada by
General Publishing Company Limited
THIRD PRINTING, SEPTEMBER, 1969

Contents

7306 '69 4.95

1

Our Migrant Farm Workers

The murky mid-August dusk is thickening as John Washington, his wife, and two children—Harry, sixteen, and Cecilia, fourteen—enter their tar-paper shack in a southern New Jersey migrant labor camp. So tired that he staggers through the doorway, John turns on the single electric light hanging from the ceiling, and the exhausted children throw themselves upon the soiled mattresses of the two squeaky beds.

Mrs. Washington draws brownish cold water from the faucets in the dirty sink and lights the two burners of the stove, whose fuel comes from cylinders outside the cabin. On one burner is hot water for washing; on the other, the evening meal, which is to be an oxtail stew with potatoes. When the bath water is hot, she will boil some beans on the burner. This evening she is too tired to prepare any of her time-consuming specialties. Since the camp toilet is some distance away, the Washingtons will use a battered tin pail which will be placed outside overnight.

All four have worked since eight o'clock that morning in a field muddy from the recent rains that had caused the Washingtons to be idle for several days. They have been kneeling in the mud for nine hours selecting and picking the riper tomatoes, and they have collected paper tickets which they will turn in to their crew leader on payday. They are trying to gather enough money to tide them over the winter months in their native Georgia. At week's end, the four together will have earned only a little over eighteen dollars for each day's toil.

The Washingtons are interstate Negro migrant farm laborers who have been harvesting various crops since mid-May, moving north from South Carolina. They have already done field work in both South and North Carolina, and in Delaware and Maryland, and will work elsewhere in New Jersey before ending their trip in New York State. Early in September the bus in which they travel with more than forty other workers will return directly to the South. They will arrive at their home base, they hope and pray, with enough money to have made the long trip worthwhile.

In central Michigan at almost the same time, Domingo Salazar, a Mexican-American, and his family of three are returning from the fields where they have been fortunate enough to obtain work picking cucumbers that will be used for pickles. The entire family—Domingo, his wife Celia, and sixteen-year-old Julio and fourteen-year-old Juanita—have worked in the hot sun since early morning.

On their knees, which have been protected by wrapped towels, they have picked the ripe cucumbers, placing them in baskets which, when full, each carries to the end of the row to be checked in and exchanged for empty baskets. Their earnings depend on the quantity of cucumbers they pick, so they take no break. Back and forth they move, with a short pause for lunch—a sandwich and a soft drink for which they pay on the spot.

Almost sick with weariness, reeking of sweat and the

smell of soil, they have returned to their two-family cabin, which costs them fifteen dollars for the week. A curtain divides the interior, on the other side of which lives another and unfamiliar family whose every word and move can be heard by them. Too fatigued to prepare a meal, Señora Salazar warms up leftovers that the family eat in silence. The evening darkness has just begun to deepen when the family fall on the two disheveled beds, having washed only superficially in the cold tap water. (The camp washhouse is located at the end of the row of cabins, and the Salazars are too tired to visit it.) The family will sink into the heavy sleep of total exhaustion, and that may restore their strength for another day of grueling labor.

The Salazar family have traveled almost a thousand miles from central Texas in their dilapidated 1959 model automobile, seeking harvest work wherever it can be found. They have picked several different crops at six farms and now, in mid-August, are nearing the end of their journey. With the scant money which will remain after their expenses have been paid, they will head south to their home base in the Rio Grande Valley. If they are lucky, they will take back about six hundred dollars to show for the many hours they have spent stooping in the fields.

Far away, in southern Colorado, the five-member family of Francisco Delgado, Mexican-Americans from Texas, are nearing the end of a long day's field work, harvesting lettuce. The two oldest children—sixteen-year-old Enrique and thirteen-year-old Elena—also work along the rows. Their third child, Carlos, six, has remained at the migrant camp, where he plays with the other young children whose families are absent for the day.

Francisco and his wife Josefina have worked eight hours together, chattering and singing, occasionally humming and talking over the activities of their hundred-odd fellow crew-members.

Under the protective guidance of their crew chief, who has made many such trips, the Delgados are at midpoint in their annual five-month journey. Eltore, their *patron* (boss), has cared for them on their long bus trip and has made certain that their quarters in the various camps were satisfactory. As a result, the Delgados and their companions in Eltore's crew have become a happy unit. Though the field work of the harvests is dreary and tiring, they know that when the long day is over they will wash up, eat well, and pass an hour or two with their friends before a night of restful sleep in the quarters provided for them, which will prepare them for the next day's work. All is *muy bueno* with them.

The widely separated families of the Washingtons, Salazars, and Delgados have one thing in common. They are twelve among the more than three hundred thousand seasonal farm laborers who annually "follow the sun" singly or in groups from the South to the rural areas of northern states where a wide variety of crops are at their peak of ripeness. Their arrivals are eagerly awaited by the growers who rely upon them for the harvests.

Within the past twenty years, the United States has been witnessing a full-scale migration that is strongly affecting the economic system of our country. More and more of the poor, mainly from the southern states, have participated in a continual and seemingly endless exodus from rural areas to the contemporary promised land—the northern cities—where, they hope, they may find work to give them a wage which will supply them with the basic necessities of life and break the bondage of poverty.

Almost ten million farmers and farm workers, both white and black, left rural areas between 1950 and 1960, and in the twenty-five years since 1942 the rural population of the United States has declined by almost 60 percent, from 29,000,000 to 11,500,000. The reason for this rural-to-urban movement has been twofold: the increased mechanization of agriculture and the phenomenal growth of a new type of farming called agribusiness or corporate farming. This particularly affected the small farmer whose limited acreage prevented his competing with larger farms in productivity, as well as eliminating the need for field hands, mainly Negroes.

As the large farms, both corporate and individually owned and operated, replaced the smaller ones, a new type of worker replaced the yearlong hired man and the field hands. These were the seasonal workers who were needed in large numbers to harvest the crops which required hand labor rather than machines.

Michael Harrington, whose book *The Other America,* published in 1962, exposed the shocking incidence of poverty under the patina of our ever-growing and affluent contemporary society, described them in these words:

> The migrant workers are not only the most obvious victims of this triumphant agricultural technology; their plight has been created by progress. In the new structure of farming, a great number of human beings are required for a brief period to do work that is too delicate for machines and too dirty for any but the dispossessed. So the Southern Negroes, the Texas-Mexicans, the California Anglos are packed like cattle into trucks and make their pilgrimage of misery.

Vegetable and fruit farmers, both corporate and individual, have become increasingly dependent upon seasonal migrant farm workers—like the Washingtons, the Salazars, and the Delgados—who leave their more or less permanent homes when needed to harvest specific crops. These migrants make up an essential part of the agricultural labor force in almost every area of our country where the demand exists for large numbers of short-term workers to do highly critical work at specific times. These periods occur when the crops must, in agricultural terms, be "gathered in," that is, handpicked and harvested, for marketing and/or processing. They differ from the vast number of migrants in the rural-to-urban movement in that they return to their homes in the South when their work has been completed.

These present-day annual migrants who work "on the season," particularly those who travel beyond the boundaries of their home states, form the subject of this book.

Migratory workers first became a significant source of seasonal labor supply during the first World War, when manpower shortages existed. In the East and Midwest, these were mainly newly arrived immigrants. At that time (and today as well) California used by far the largest number of migrant workers, both native-born Americans and Mexican *braceros* who were imported for short periods in increasing numbers at very low wages.

But beginning in the Depression years of the mid-1930's, California was besieged by an invasion from the Midwest— the displaced farmers of the dust bowl who needed work for their survival. Between 1933 and 1939, 350,000 were said to have arrived. Unlike the Mexicans, they intended to become permanent residents. In the widespread misery of the Depression years, the poor and unemployed were everywhere, and most Americans were unaware of the plight of these newcomers in California. But a book served to awaken the conscience of the country and to focus national attention on all migrant workers.

The book was a work of fiction, John Steinbeck's *The Grapes of Wrath,* published in April, 1939. It immediately became "the book of the season, the year, possibly the decade," and is still among the most widely read American novels. The book's subject is the odyssey of the Joads, a family of three generations, dispossessed from their Oklahoma farm in the dust bowl and seeking field and orchard work—any farm work at all—after their arrival in California, only to be driven from camp to camp there. Steinbeck, who lived in the Salinas Valley, skillfully pictured the Joads as the victims of the Depression and as examples of the desperate work-seekers everywhere.

The immediate result was to focus the attention of the nation on migrants and their treatment. Investigations by committees of both the United States Senate and the House of Representatives followed. Mrs. Eleanor Roosevelt visited the camps and talked with individual migrants, corroborating the tragic picture painted in words by Mr. Steinbeck.

Government agencies, both federal and state, began to turn their belated attention to the problem of the wandering workers wherever they were employed seasonally. This continuing attention, however, was slow in bringing about reforms, and little change on the national level occurred until 1962 and 1963, when the first major legislation was enacted (Chapter 12). By that time many states had undertaken official inquiries, and some had passed their own laws and established standards. But the effectiveness of a statute or regulation depends on its enforcement, and only within recent years has any significant improvement in the condition of the seasonal workers' lives taken place.

The majority of migrant workers are still all too often exploited and deprived of the basic rights enjoyed by the average American. As members of minority groups, they are frequently dominated by heartless and unfeeling supervisors and farmers. They perform the most menial of work in all kinds of weather—under the scorching sun, and in the mud following torrential rains, when their picking must be hurried lest the particular field crop be ruined and lost. They often travel in acute discomfort and live near their places of work in unsanitary, rundown, and crowded quarters. Further, and in spite of a mass of federal and state legislation, they are generally ineligible for minimum wages, workmen's compensation, and temporary disability and unemployment insurance. They are not eligible to vote. When stranded far from their homes, they are often unable to obtain public assistance payments. Like all farm workers, they have not yet been accepted for membership in labor unions except in a few isolated and pioneer instances. They remain the victims of hopelessness, even despair.

Every year in the late spring and early summer months, literally thousands of buses, often dilapidated inside and out, move northward on our nation's major arterial highways. Additional thousands of automobiles, almost always used cars and often models of a decade or more past, join the flow, always in a northerly direction. Though not readily identifiable in the interstate traffic on the highways and turnpikes, they are a familiar—and welcome—sight on the less-traveled local roads in the rural areas where the largest farms are located. Often their destination is reached by secondary unpaved and dusty roads.

The growers await their arrival with eager anticipation. Plans have long been made for the harvest dates, and when the pickers arrive the farmers hope that the season will be financially profitable and realize that these seasonal workers are essential to such success.

The harvesters have often traveled several hundred, or even a thousand, miles, to remain in the vicinity perhaps only a few days, possibly several weeks. They arrive singly and in groups, in buses and automobiles. Very often, large and small families—including the very young and sometimes the very old who are still strong and active enough to perform the grueling and punishing field work—travel together. When the harvests are completed, they move farther north—always northward—to new fields in which a bountiful crop awaits and needs them.

By the end of the season, some of these interstate farm migrants, though far from their southern home bases, return directly to them. Others make their return southward with stops where the crops of late summer or early fall are still to be harvested. An almost identical travel pattern may be followed from year to year, with the laborers working in the same or nearby localities, picking the same or different vegetables or fruits.

This flow of seasonal farm workers follows three established patterns or streams: the Atlantic Coast, the Central, and the Pacific Coast. Two of these streams, the first and the third, are characterized by one main line, a broad strip or belt. Because it covers a wider area, the Central Stream has several northward main belts or paths with abundant branches to the east and west. These streams are based on the location of the major crops to be worked. The map on page 171 shows the geographical coverage of these streams. Appendix III describes the time coverage and the types of crops harvested.

The taped interviews with migrants working in the three streams (Chapters 2, 3, and 4) present these wandering workers as human beings, with the conditions they encounter in their work and lives; the good and bad features which make them either happy or miserable, the planning for their annual trips, their adjustment to the migrant life, and their restlessness and hopes.

Migrants pose a statistical problem: no one knows exactly how many of them there are. As an observer has remarked, the Government takes a census of migrant birds but not of migrant human beings. Statistics compiled by the Bureau of Employment Security of the United States Department of Labor for 1965, admittedly incomplete, are included in the table in Appendix II. Some analysis is made in Chapter 3. Definitions of the various types of workers appear in Appendix I.

Like all workers in various occupations in our country, migratory workers present vast differences in their racial backgrounds and their attitudes toward life. Yet they share one common aim, a simple and basic one: they want to earn a living wage; and to obtain this objective they are willing to undergo the inconveniences and hardships of life in strange surroundings far from their home bases.

The workers following the three major streams and their subsidiary branches continue to supply a large part of the necessary seasonal-labor work force. As the Migrant Ministry of the National Council of Churches in the United States points out, "Because of the labor of the migrant's hands, his endless steps climbing up and down ladders, his stooping and digging into the earth, his plucking and picking from vines and branches, there are fruits and vegetables on our tables this day."

Here, then, are pictures of the lives of those who follow the crops northward "on the season" in different parts of our country.

2

On the Season:
The Atlantic Coast Stream

The annual flow of migrant farm workers from the South up the Atlantic coast occurs like clockwork. When the caravans of buses and automobiles arrive, work begins almost immediately, for the mature crops are in their prime, and the schedules have been planned in detail. The subjects of these case studies represent all types of interstate migrants.

The Lee family, for example, are veterans who are solidly booked by an efficient and kindly crew leader. The Smiths, as workers without any definite plans, show the futility and frustration of those—all too many—who find themselves aimlessly traveling from place to place, led by rumor and dependent upon chance to find the work which is so essential to them. Mrs. Louise Jones is a contented "single" crew member who, as an experienced specialist, has long since adjusted to the migrant way of life. Bill Allen is a "loner" traveling with a crew of singles, who in his own opinion has found satisfaction in the annual trips. The contrasts between them are apparent.

Here, then, are four followers of the Atlantic Coast Stream.

A Family on the Move

Abraham Lincoln Lee is a stocky Negro from central Georgia who has worked "on the season" for about fifteen years. He is probably in his mid-forties and brings his wife and the oldest four of his seven children, who range from five to seventeen, with him each year. The three youngest remain in the Georgia cabin under the care of his mother-in-law, who sees that they attend school "regular." While he is away an assortment of relatives, both male and female, work his small fields. His work as a migrant laborer apparently makes it possible to have a "good life" (his expression). In fact, these earnings form the largest share of his annual income.

His adored wife Mattie is obviously the family manager. Having the advantage of seven years of pre-marriage schooling, she can read and write and therefore keeps the records and "holds" the money. She is a loyal, devoted wife and mother who wants the best for her children.

Abe went to school for only two years; then it became necessary for him to "do a man's work." As a result he is almost completely illiterate, and his speech lacks even the most basic elements of grammar. His pronunciation is often muddled, and the words he uses only approximate their proper forms. As can be seen, however, he is a splendidly proud Negro, uncomplaining yet not too easygoing. He will stand up for what he thinks is right and will see that promises are kept. He expects to earn the money he receives by doing his work carefully and satisfactorily. (Many migrant workers are content to do only what is basically necessary in order to receive the hourly or day wage; this is why piecework is often preferred by farmers because of its incentive value.)

Mike Bishop, Abe's crew leader (Chapter 6), pays tribute to his devotion in these words: "Abe is about the best they come. I say that because a crew boss makes contracts to do a certain amount of work, and if his crew does not meet these promises he gets a black eye with the growers and may not be welcome the next year. I can always count on him. He never makes problems and never misbehaves. He is a good family man, and they are the best workers because they feel an obligation toward their wives and children. Of course, this works two ways: by treating him right and playing square with him, he will work well for me. Perhaps this is a selfish way of operating, but it *does* pay off."

Abe's experience as a migrant worker is not completely typical; instead of being confined to "stoop" labor (in his case, tomato picking), he also works in what is sometimes called "upright" labor (tree-picking on ladders; in his case, apples, cherries, and peaches). He bears testimony to the physical satisfaction in these work variations.

The following taped interview was made early in September, 1967, at a tomato farm in southern New Jersey. This was one of the farms cited by the state Task Force (Chapter 8) as having "deplorable, even scandalous, housing and living conditions," in almost complete disregard of the state standards and regulations. Fortunately for Abe Lee, this was one of the few times in his extensive migrant experience that he was thus victimized.

Here is his story.

Tell me about yourself and your life before you followed the crops.

I is a cullud man bawn in Gawgia. I is not 'zackly sure how old I is 'cuz I ain't registeered—I found that out when they aksed me my age when I first begin to come nawth. But I guess I be about forty-odd or mebbe more 'cuz I remembers the 'Pression [Depression] when I was mebbe nine or ten.

My name? Well, the "Lee" come from the gin'ral of the [Civil] war. Long ago, it seem, my granddaddy and grand-mammy wuz slaves, and their massa pick that las' name 'cuz he like the gin'ral good. My first names come from good ole Abe who done so much for free the slaves.

My daddy wuz a Gawgia sharecropper with a little piece of lan' he wuk for a white man who owned it. They wuz sev'ral nigguh families what had they fields and they cabins, and earned 'cordin' to what they turned in each year. I was pickin' cotton when six year old, with my brudders and sisters. This was before the machines come which done our wuk. After dat we did not need to tote them big bags and break our backs (cotton-pickin' is lots of leanin').

We also chops cotton when the plants was agrowin' ["chopping" is weeding and thinning with a hoe]. Sometimes we also picks peaches—them's bestest of all fruits—and gits lots of hurt ones or ones that has spots of rotten brown and we sure did stuff our stomachs, and the wimmens jars [cans] 'em and we has 'em year 'roun.

My wife Mattie and me was spliced when I was sixteen; she was fifteen. We lives on the garden and we wuks the little land piece and me and my brudders and sisters picks cotton after August 'til the frost 'bout midst of October. We also picks for farmers variously, like tobacco, peanuts, and cotton. Cotton not too hard 'cuz the bags is light and theys no need to stoop, but de pay is little and de sun is hot. I like the cawn, too, 'cuz you stand up, tho' the bags is soon heavy. Sometime we travels to pick peaches; we is on ladders, and we has to be kerful in handle 'em. The childrens does vegetables and they gets tired easy leanin' over.

Well, my childrens comes regular, and by ten year we has

five which my missus has alone. For one she has akchully in a field wid the other wimmens helpin' her. Meanwhiles de house was too little, and three, four brudders and sisters goes nawth wid theys famblies to live. Finally we has de cabin is ours alone. We has two udder childrens later.

One day 'bout fifteen year back (my missus keep de records as she go to school a little before we be splice), a nigguh man come by, and he say "Abe, how come you stay right here? They is money in travel and you sees the outside. You nevah gets ahead here. You signs with me and I promises good money and you follows the crops to de nawth."

Well, we talks a lots and since we has some money set by, we buys an ole Ford from a man what die. It not look like nuthin' but it run. We be on the road mosta time since part of year, but we comes back home for winter 'cuz it be warmer there and dey no fields work our kinds nawth after 'bout Thanksgivin'.

What about your travels and work, especially this trip?

Mike—that he name—sign me and my childrens (sometimes they wuks, sometimes not), and give money to get to places, which we pays back. Afterwards we pays our own way. They is also some buses even with famblies and we goes alone 'til we meets them. We never goes to but three-four place on each trip nawth, mebbe five if we has wuk when we makes the trip back south to Gawgia.

Yes, we is crew member even tho's we travels lonely; only diff'rence is we is not in the buses, it be better that way wid childrens.

Where we go? This-here year we go five place only, three on way up nawth, two on way back home. We do that next we leave here [New Jersey].

Since Mike fix us up we does only speshul crops; these is sometimes diff'rent each year. This trip we does several speshuls.

The crew members, about eighty-five, traveled in two buses; several families like the Lees went along in automobiles. Mike Bishop traveled in one of the buses. The Lees joined the rest in South Carolina, near the Atlantic Ocean, in mid-May to pick tomatoes for four weeks. The last two weeks of June found them on the Maryland Eastern Shore, again with tomatoes. During the month of July they picked cherries in the Hudson River Valley of New York. From early August to mid-September tomatoes were again picked, this time in southern New Jersey. They moved to three different localities in two counties in one of which, Cumberland, the interview was taped. From there they were scheduled to return to the Hudson River Valley, this time to pick apples for a fortnight. For six weeks, from early October to mid-November, on the return trip south, they would be in western Virginia harvesting the late apple crop and, perhaps, peaches.

The family will be back at their Georgia home the last of November, and they will then take over the working of the land from their relatives. This will be mostly their own crops, with occasional days of work (not harvesting) nearby. Mike will get in touch with them in late March or early April after he has firmed his commitments to Northern growers.

Abe again:

They is also lotsa peoples what picks only speshuls, and sometimes they wuks wid us, though mos'ly they is in groups what wuks togedder. If they is near us and them beans is not ready they joins us for 'til they can do de beans. Some of de Florida wukkers does only snap beans, which is hard to pick 'cuz they is many on de same plant, and some is ready and big and some is weensy and ungrown.

You aks about which pickings is hardest and which we likes best. Tomatoes is hard 'cuz not all is jes' ripe when we goes down de rows. Some is green and little, and we stops to look and takes only de ready ones. Mike has learnt us what to do. Some places where we been in tomatoes does not need us no more 'cuz they has some machines. Trouble wid tomatoes is dat some is ripe 'mos all the time, and it depend on de weather, and sometimes we goes over and over down de rows to ketch the later ripe ones. We wuks in pairs, and one pick and one put in boxes and kerry de boxes to man at end of row who check off what we do, for pay. Tomatoes is also easy hurt and we has to be kerful not to drop 'em if dey goes to market; if dey is for canning, which is sometimes, it don' matter 'cuz they is not have to be perfec'.

Cherries is not so bad 'cuz there no stooping, and it more easy on back and we not so tired at end of day (sometimes I jes' drops when I gets home at night and I is too tired to even eat 'til I rests). We wuks on ladders, sometimes high, but I not get dizzy like some.

We gets balance on ladder and reaches out 'til all is pick, then moves ladder to next side of tree. We moves from top to bottom to get all cherries and puts them in buckets on a nail; when these-here buckets is full someone below (sometimes my boy) give an empty one and take the full one away to check in and get credit. The leaning in cherries pickin' is not too bad, and it good after the tomatoes. We takes kere to keep stems on if they is fer market; if they is fer canning we does not kere fer eggzakness 'cuz the fact'ry does the stems when they takes out de pits.

Apples is 'bout de same only de pails (sometimes baskets) fills up quicker and is heavy. Most times they is for market, so we again watches kereful. They does not always be entire ripe. Sometimes we does not pick, but since we is there we helps wid packing in cases after they is cleaned. Dis good for back and arms to rest, and we does better when we goes back to pickin'.

Peaches is like tomatoes in some ways, depend on ripenesses. If dis is hard, all o.k. 'cept we is kereful always not to hurt if they for market. Mike always tell us 'bout dis.

For all dese pickins they is always some which is part bad. We puts 'em togedder 'cuz when dey is sorted later they is sep'rated. This is 'cuz some shoppers looks at all and takes only dose best ones. But we jes' picks and puts 'em togedder.

The childrens? I lets 'em wuk only when it not too hard or when dey is special needed. Of course, they is not so fast but Mattie not want 'em be too tired. Lots famblies lets children get overtired and theys health is not good. We—Mattie and me —figgers we want keep 'em well; the money not wuth they health. They is good at totin' 'less the loads is too heavy. One take each end and wuks togedder so's neither have too heavy load. They stops when they is tired and goes back to rest.

Money? Las' year we clears 'bout one thousand one hundred dollars on de trip, but dis include de children wuk. Dis trip so far I gets 'bout eight dollah day and wuks six-day week. Childrens wuks 'bout four day week, get four dollah day. So mebbe we takes back 'bout de same after all 'spenses paid. [This is for the six-months trip and depends on the prices of lodging and food, which vary. Most migrants are fortunate if they can clear $700; those who have encountered hard luck, weather troubles, and poor scheduling might end up with between three and four hundred dollars and proportionately less for shorter trips. Some of the New Jersey workers were planning to return south in mid-September, and a hundred fifty to two hundred dollars appeared to be their average profit for the three months' work, again a testimony to the lack of a responsible crew leader.]

What do you think about your crew leader?

Mike, you mean? He a true good man in all ways (he a nigguh like me). I go with him now for 'leven year and to tell de truth he never do me nor my family no wrong. He not like some others we hear 'bout and them as hired me some year back. First, he keep the promises and 'greements. He good as his word, and he play fair. He promise the gas money 'stead o' say like some bosses, "I give you thirty dollar and you pay any more," and the nigguhs who is got to get to where they is work has to pay de rest, and oftentimes that a lot, 'specially if trip is farrer than dey 'spected. I knows mens who has had to pay three-four times what they gets at first 'cuz they has to go where de boss say, and at the end of season theys no better off and has to spend theys pay to get back south. Sometimes they has to borrow from him and pay back from wukking there and he charge a lot extry.

But Mike believe what we say—gas, oil, which my missus write down (she write and additions better'n me). She also write down de miles. But we does have to pay for tires and speshul repairs 'cuz dat is part of our 'spenses. The mens who travels in buses without famblies is paid for, and jes' goes 'long.

My boss stop in when we is settled in de houses, and look 'round and aks us is we comfort and happy. He aks 'bout cooking and even toilets. And couple times like here he say to de farmer, "These peoples no work 'lessen they has some comfort." Sometime the farmer say, "Take it or leave it," and he say to us, "Wait overnight and mebbe I finds 'nother place nearby," and sure 'nuff next day he come back and say, "Go 'long to Mr. Jones, he have beans (or 'spargus or tomatoes or somepin' like) to pick and tell him who you is. Say I has sent you, and he make you real comfort." Then he stop by if it not too far to be sure we not be cheated on de pay and to collect on us. All time he keep track of us fambly.

Sometime he say, "Your childrens is tired. They not wuk no more for awhile," and he give a name in a town, and he say, "You drive dere and your childrens get fixed for summer school and you can take 'em each mornin' before you goes to de field, and you can pick 'em up nights to be wid you." One time my son Rafe here [*pointing*] get right sick and go wid us to state doctor to get well. All the childrens gets de shots and sometimes Mike help us get clothes and shoes when we not have money. He say that better than stay alone all day in de house. Sometime he talk 'bout theys schooling be better than the moneys they can earn.

Yes, he just a good man and he know we honest and he take good care us. He not tat all like mos' boss. They is mean and theys only wants de monies they gets fer getting de wukkers for theys farmers.

Oh, yes, he do one speshul thing. When the government security [social security] is come in action, he writes de papers and see my missus and I is paid for by de farmer-boss. This is so we not work forever, and we pays some, too. Lotsa boss pay no 'tenshun to these-here rights and lotsa peoples knows

nothing 'bout it and when we tells 'em they goes to theys boss
and he play dumb and say, "What you mean? That don't go
for you. You has no number and 'til you gets one you is not
'vailable [eligible]." They just does not want to bother.

Yes, my Mike boss is want to keep us happy 'cuz he know
we all wuks better then. Suh, we nigguhs is no diff'rent dat
way than yous whites.

What about your places to live [to Mrs. Lee]?

We have had some troubles with places to stay, but more
often good times. Since we travel in the auto we want to stay
together as a family, and we don't want to be too close to
others. Though we make some friends, our stays are so short
that we do not get very close. However, it is nice for the children to be with others of their own ages. Mike usually takes
care of us, so it is very often good. When it is bad, we talk
to him and keep our mouths tight shut with the owners so that
we will not become known as troublemakers. Complaining to
them does no good; in many cases the farmers just don't care,
because they know we are only temporary and will be moving
on. I think Mike complains to the state people, because once
in a while when we have returned to the same place the next
year the conditions have been better.

I understand farmers can now get some loans from the government, and these new places are sometimes of cement, which
is cold at night, but at least the floors are good. There are no
bugs and there have even been fairly new stoves that really
work. One place even had gas in bottles; mostly we have piles
of wood near the door, and I am used to making fires; Abe
says I am the best firemaker he ever knew of [*laughs*]!

When I get to a new place, before we unload (we carry
cooking stuff—pots and pans, a teakettle, blankets, and bed
things) I always go in first to get a good look before we settle
down. I can see right away if anything is wrong. Sometimes
there is not enough space to move around in since the beds take
up lots of room for us six people. The children you see are
Eliza (twelve), Charles ('most fourteen), Betsy (fifteen and a
half), and my oldest son Rafe (seventeen). You see, most of

our children are alternate girls and boys, but we did not plan it that way [*laughs*]! At one of the state places about five years ago they asked me did I want babies every so often, regular like, and then I said, "Well, not exactly, but they *do* come, you know." The lady nurse said, "Wouldn't it be better for your work on these trips if you were not pregnant? Because then you could help more and not have to watch your strength." and she told me what to do. By good luck, *not* planning, I have had my children at home in Georgia, but, yes, it did make me have to be careful and I could not work and earn much when the time came near. Taking care of Abe and the children and the places we had was all I could and should do, and I had regular examinations at nice, clean clinics, but never a baby in them [*laughs*]. This nurse gave me information [birth control] and it has worked well. I like a big family, but more babies would keep me at home. The children at home are between five and about eleven and my mother sees that they go to school and not work too much, just help in weeding and such. Negro children expect to work and share the work load.

In the one room we have to have three double beds: the girls sleep together, the boys together, so I first look for that, because workers must have their rest. Lordy, half a dozen times in the past we had only one double bed and two singles, and it was not at all comfortable, but we made the best of it.

Then I look in the corners and under the beds, which have only mattresses, to see if there are any roaches and bugs; if we find any I use the spray right off. Walls with peeling paint also have roaches; sometimes I look at the mattresses to be sure there are no bedbugs, because, Lordy, they are *awful!* One time we had a terrible time with them for three weeks because they are hard to find except from the bites. You get up quick, turn on the light, and quick kill them if at all possible.

Next I look at the stove and the water. Sometimes the faucets give only a little stream or are broken, and that means Rafe has to fetch water from the outdoor pumps or faucets in a bucket we carry. If the floor is dirty, I mop and scrub it right away.

Then I look at the toilets and wash places. This is almost always bad. The toilets may be far away, quite a walk, and people are not very careful, and sometimes they are really filthy and sickening. Ugh! Once in a while the women get together and clean it out (most of them are not afraid of work), but they seem to be almost always dirty within a day. I have to have good clean water for both cooking and washing. We carry a big basin for the clothes, which have to be washed regular else they get so dirty you can never get them clean. Abe laughs at how much clothes I have hanging around (we carry a clothes-line and pins). I have learned never to do washing in damp or rainy weather, but wait for a sunny day. Sometimes I hang inside, sometimes out. I almost always use warm water for dishes because the foods we eat have lots of grease and fat. Abe calls me a fat-fighter [*laughs*].

For light there is generally only one hanging bulb in the center. Sometimes it is not very good, but we have learned to carry a big strong one which we use and take away with us. We do not have electricity in our Georgia home, so it is better in these places.

On the whole we manage to make out. Yes, things are better for the last few years because of the new state laws. Most of the farmers seem to feel like Mike does, that we work better when we are happy in our houses.

Lordy, one thing that happens often that I don't like. This is when a one-room house has to be shared with another family. Sometimes we get acquainted with another family we like and that travels in the same crew, either by their auto or in the bus. Then it is real sociable and like one big family. But very often there is a family from another crew that we don't know, and then we just grin and bear it. We do not get friendly until we get to know them and their ways. If it works out nice we have good times and the women and children help each other.

When two families are in the same house, it works two ways. There may be a thin barrier [partition] dividing it in two, or there may be a curtain in the middle which we draw when we want to be alone. If the other family is noisy, we have to make the best of it, but it is a part of our living.

On this trip we have been lucky. In South Carolina it was not so good, but we make do. Maryland was good (there were some big divided houses with our own front doors and steps).

New York was fine, and this here not so good comparisonly. We pay about five dollars a week (one day's pay), never more, seldom less. We expect to pay this. Mike collects from everyone and pays the farmer.

Tell me about your food [to Mrs. Lee].

You will laugh, but we eat very simple things, not fancy, but what we are used to. We have to eat well to do the work, but I have learned to feed the family on an allowance [budget]. Lordy, in meats we special [-ize] in pork (fried), oxtails, pig-tails, pig's feet and the like. I often have good beef bones which I make into fine soups; they fill up the belly quickly with good vitameens when I add vegetables (of course lots of to-matoes) [*laughs*]. We have chitlings when we can get them (not in the north), but the northern people must throw them away because I cannot find them very often. They sure are missing something [*laughs*]!

Yes, most meat is pork in the cheaper pieces because other meats cost too much. But sometimes we celebrate birthdays and good times with roasts and tongues which can be used for sandwiches and more meals. But it hurts to pay so much, really it does.

We eat lots of rice, grits, cornmeal, and sweet potatoes or yams. Salads and desserts, never. We feed for strength, not for fanciness or sweet tooths. Of course we eat the fruits and vegetables we pick (the bad ones they give us free). I use lots of flour for biscuits and gravies which adds flavor. We never have butter; Lordy, it is too much money and does not keep, (there are never any iceboxes and the weather is hot so it is too hard to keep some things from spoiling).

We buy as we need things, almost every day. There are usu-ally stores [company or cooperatives] in one of the buildings in the biggest camps, and we charge everything and pay just before we leave, sometimes with the work tickets they give us, often with actual money.

The tickets? This is the way the farmer keeps track of what work we do. At the end of each day Abe brings back these slips of paper, and I keep them all and we get cash before we leave. Yes, we can use them while we are there. If the children want a treat like a cold drink of something—once in a long while some candy—I give them a ticket and they bring back the money. Lordy, they deserve a treat once in a while.

None of us like to carry money in camp or have it in the house since one time about four years ago we were robbed while in the fields—all the money so far was under a mattress and no one told us that was the first place a thief would look. We learned that the hard way—$86 the hard way. Now we always have it on us. Abe has a special zip [zipper] pocket and I have a special-made pocket in my skirt with a big safety pin. No one rob no more from a Lee [*laughs*]!

Oh, yes, on weekends or evenings we can go to a near town to buy food, and there is a big supra [super] market (which we do not have near us in Georgia). We buy lots and save money. We pack what is left in a box in the back of the auto and take it with us.

One good thing: we do not smoke or drink, and this saves lots of money. I know some workers who are always owing because of this. That is something to be thankful for.

What about the children who are with you [to Mrs. Lee]?

As I told you, we have been bringing our four oldest with us for two years, since Eliza was ten and Rafe fifteen. Maybe I made a mistake in starting out with them when they were so young, because we began bringing Rafe when he was twelve, that time alone. Lordy, if it were to start again I would wait until they were perhaps thirteen, then they would have more school, which we now want them to have.

The children I worry about lots, but the reason I bring them along is that I just can't ask my mother to care for so many, and three is about all she can handle and keep in order. These youngest in Georgia go to an all-colored school—the mixing rule does not go in our county in spite of the law; there are always some excuses, and, besides, this is the nearest, only two miles from home.

Lordy, now you are right ready to ask me why, if I put such a store on schooling, I take the oldest ones with us. Part it is because of what I said about my mother, and part is because we don't want to leave them all for such a long time. It is better to keep some of us together lest the older ones get independence ideas and decide they are grown up before they really are. Even now Rafe is wanting to stay in the north with his aunts and uncles; not like some who have left, they work hard and make good livings and seem happy and better off up there in, let's see, Chicago, Detroit and New York. But we have promised Rafe that when he is a man (he says eighteen, we say twenty-one) he can go, and maybe he will get a job and go to night school and make up for what he has lost in school work. Poor people cannot always choose what they know is best for their children, you know.

These children you see with me—Eliza, Charles, Betsy and Rafe—do get some school from when we get back just before Thanksgiving until we leave again in May. The school is fixed in two groups and the teachers are used to the pupils being gone—lots of being away for farm work, picking, cotton chopping, and the like. In these classes lotsa children work different [on different levels] and they make out as best they can. They always have reading, learning to write, and doing sums and numbers. What they lose is things like history and poems and such, but they can't get everything.

Now, on the trips as Abe told you, we don't let them work all the time, even though, Lord knows, we want to make as much money as we can so that they can have things back home. Well, sometimes the farmers do not let the younger children work. The government, I understand, does not want any child under sixteen to do field work, except after school. But some states we cover have their own rules. Of course, for the summer months there is often no school anyways, so we have only to think about May and part of June, and in September and October. Some places have special summer schools, but not often where we have ever been.

This here trip? When we were in South Carolina, the first stop, they picked tomatoes with us because there is no rule, and they was fresh from school and not yet tired. By the time we got to Maryland there was no school, so they all worked off and on, depending on how they felt. Same for here [New Jersey]. When we go back to New York for two weeks probably none will work because that state is very strict and even

the two oldest would have to get special permissions [permits],
so all except Rafe will probably go to school, even if it is for
so little time [two weeks]. We know the school and it is like
a rest for them anyway.

But I must say it is not good and happy for them because
they are strangers and the regular children are 'way ahead.
But it is the law. In Virginia there are some rules which Mike
and the state people will tell us about, and probably the three
youngest will go to school and work only part time. This is a
long time [six weeks] so it is better that they not work so much
because by that time they have done their share, and we really
want them to get ready for the Georgia school. That longer
time they will be more comfort with the strange boys and
girls, so we think it good. Lordy, it is a problem, though.

How do they get along? Well, it is different one to the other.
Eliza always settles down and is happy, but Charles is funny.
He feels so to be a stranger, you know, and it depends the
teacher. Boys, 'specially strangers, have more trouble than
girls. Depends on the school, I guess. Mike introduces us—he
is always good that way—and I keep them clean so they not
get looked at as funny children. Sometimes Charles have fights
with teasers, but Abe says [and she imitates her husband without sarcasm, but with exactness to make her point], "Looky
here, boy, at your papa. See how he not been to school. See
how he talk bad and how he work so hard. It not be that way
with his childrens if they be schooled," and they understand.
They are not ashamed of him because they have respect and
he treats them always nice. Of course, we rather have them
in one school all the time, but I explained that, didn't I?

One thing I don't like. They have few friends along the way
except those in our crew. Naturally, they get acquainted with
some, so they are not too lonely. It is not the best, we know
that, but it has to do.

Do you meet many local people [to Mrs. Lee]?

You mean in the towns near where we work? Lordy, we are
so close that we have enough with each other without much
socializing. But we do have Saturday nights and Sundays when
we want to get away from where we are.

Come-and-go workers like us have different welcomes in different towns. Very often, 'specially in Maryland and New York and a couple of times in New Jersey places, there are real welcomes, with special attention given to us. They have dances and parties for the grownups, with eats, and sometimes movies and even live plays. When we go to those special parties, which we are specially invited by someone who comes out to the camp personal-like [personally], we get dressed up and washed spick-and-span so they will be glad they asked us. We carries sets of clothes for when we go to towns.

They treat the Negroes just like the whites; though we are all colored in our crew, some white crew people will be there, too, and perhaps some foreigners [Puerto Ricans]. Sometimes they are in churches [parish houses] and they do not ask whether we belong (we are Baptists back home). At first we were suspecting and uneasy, but we were wrong. In some of our groups there are people who play geetars and mouth organs, and who sing all sorts of songs, and who dance, and sometimes our own people give the entertaining. Ofttimes we thank them with a show of our own. When we go on from these places, we are really sorry because we have been so happy outside of the work.

For the children there are special things in some towns; the only trouble is that we can't always tote them there. They have been to playgrounds, with slides and swings and things we do not have down south, and there are games and sports. Betsy learned to sew—better than me!—in four weeks in one town, I think it was in New York last year.

Many towns are nice for children, specially for the real young ones, which myself I don't think should be brought on these trips because they can't work and have to stay in camp, alone if the mother works or with an older girl to care for them. This is no way for young children, but in some towns there are nurseries [day care] where a mother can leave the children when she works. Also all children can visit the health places [clinics] and get medicine to get well. New York and Maryland is special good for this; you can take the older children even for all day and this is good, because a mother can work without worrying. Of course, in most camps there are mothers who do not work, and for a little money they will watch your children while you are in the fields.

There are some health places with no cost. The children even get shots by the white ladies [nurses] against diseases. One time my young Betsy here, when she was twelve, have the mumps late and instead of us all being shut up [quarantined] she stayed with them until the swelling went down. Another time one of the boys breaks out with spots [measles] and he stays with them and we were very happy 'bout it.

Altogether, these town things make us very happy. Lotsa workers do not want to socialize, but we do, and we like it.

Do you think you will come north again next year [to Mr. Lee]?

Of cawse. We have did it for so long that we is 'customed. We knows what to expect, and always tries hard. If we stays on the farm we not have many good things and when the childrens grow older they will want to leave, so we can take along the others; always we will have childrens with us. Mebbe we change from tomatoes or such things as I get so very tired from leaning over. But, anyway, when Mike come 'long next spring, I sign up again.

As may be seen, Abraham Lincoln Lee and family, unlike most migrant workers, are veterans. The majority of workers make no more than three successive seasonal trips north, but the Lees have made fifteen annual trips. With the help of Mike, an excellent crew leader, they appear to have accepted the life with its hardships and its joys. Life "on the season" has become their way of life for six months of every year.

A Family of Freewheelers

The 1967 trip northward as migrant workers was the second for Negro George Smith and his wife and two children, who traveled both times in a battered 1952 model Ford with an assortment of their possessions. He is a thirty-five-year-old Alabaman who entered the Atlantic Coast Stream as a freewheeler, with a minimum of knowledge of the conditions he would encounter without the guidance and protection he would have had as a crew member. In fact, he had no knowledge of such an arrangement, and set out in 1966 with little information concerning his destinations and work. He had heard stories of the wages paid and of the need for workers, and assumed that he would readily find field work as soon as he was on his way.

George is a man who possesses no outstanding physical characteristics which might set him apart. His obvious assets are a willingness, even eagerness, to work, a drive to earn money, and a wish, thus far unrealized, to change his former life. He is almost completely illiterate.

His wife Clara is equally ordinary in appearance, but soon indicates that she is the morale builder in their discouraging situation. She seems somewhat timid in speaking, and this impression may have been made because she wants to bolster her husband's flagging spirits by letting him use words in expressing to a stranger the feelings he had hesitated to reveal to her. She is apparently a devoted mother to the children with them (four have remained in Alabama).

Neither speaks at length or in detail unless encouraged. At first they seem ill at ease, but they are soon direct and straightforward in their answers. However, George's thoughts are expressed in more or less disjointed phrases rather than full sentences.

The experiences of the Smiths vividly show that the lives of migrant workers, particularly those on their own, can be filled with worry, disappointment, and frustration, and, saddest of all, can be killing to the human spirit. George and Clara Smiths exist all too often in the Atlantic Coast Stream.

The interview was taped in a camp at Cheriton, Virginia, during mid-September. The author visited this area after *The Washington Post* had exposed camps in two counties in the southern part of the state (Chapter 8). When the United States Department of Labor ruled them ineligible for federal recruiting by its Farm Labor Bureau, the growers recruited their own workers for the potato, snap bean, and sweet pepper harvests. The Smiths were hired at that time. Because their automobile was their home, they were heartily welcomed.

Tell me something about yourself [with added frequent leading questions: to Mr. Smith].

I live all my life in a little crossroad [settlement] in Alabamy, it ain't hardly on no map but it be Tuskoosa [Tuscaloosa, in eastern-central Alabama near the Mississippi state line]. This be the place where there much right [civil rights] trouble last few year. Ain't much dere. But we have little shanty [one room] with porch and steps near de road and I wuk a little piece land, not much but keep body togedder. Do odd job 'roun, too, like chop cotton in spring and pick in fall. Only udder thing is peach pickin' which we miss last two year we be on these here trip. We get 'leef [relief] and food from county, but this not 'nuff for to live.

School? No much, not 'nuff, only two-three year. Too far off to go. Marry, me 'n Clara? Yes, 'bout twelve year back. Six childs come reg'lar, four oldest back dere wid my sistah. Two wid us is youngest, this here gal, Marie, three year—bow to the white gemman, Marie—and Claude, 'most five. They is come wid us las' year, too. Four plenty for sistah to care of.

Not nuthin' else to tell. I jes' ordinary nigguh try to get 'long.

How did you happen to leave home on these trips north?

Well, nuthin' happen roun' home. We poor and mizzable. Don't have 'nuff eats, bad close, childs all sickly. 'Leef [relief] not 'nuff. There be gas pump near, an' one day car stop, peepuls get out an' buy cold drink, sit 'roun and talk. I be there. Tell story how they cum from trip up nawth work in fields, make much money, now back home to Miss'ippi. They say man cum roun' and hire 'em. See differd places, wuks in 'matoes, beans, and sech. Say if I not like it there I go, too.

Clara and me talk 'bout leavin'. No man never come by, but we know there work. Question is how get dere; we not know where go, what do. 'Nother man pass tell us get otto and start, soon find wuk. Borrow moneys from kuzin, promise pay when back. Old car, low price. Gather stuff we need, send for sistah stay wid childs. Drive off May to get wuk. Ask 'long way, still no wuk. Go 'long, 'long ways and money get low. Finally hear tell of farm need help. This is Ca'lina, pick 'matoes three week for three dollah day. Jes' save us. Then on nawth and pick beans two week. Then wander roun', no wuk for long, mebbe 'nother two week. Finally in Ginny wuk off'n on res' of hot months. Turn back home wid $60. Pretty good but not as 'spected. That las' year.

What about this trip? Where have you been and what have you picked?

I disremember 'zackly. Clara mebbe tell.

(Mrs. Smith): All right. We start out in May 'gain and this time we more prepared. We declare there be no trouble no more. Somehow it not work out again too well, so far at least. We go fust direct to Ca'lina, same places we wuz las' year. We go roun' an' roun' again, then find work two week in 'matoes. This it at—reckon I don't 'member the place. [The Smiths failed to recall the name of but one locality of the many they had visited in both years. When asked about this, Mrs. Smith said, "All places are same, most we want to fergit; we not stay very long and get all mixed [up] by goin' roun' so many place."] Gawge wuk, me have to kere for Marie and Claude, they too young be lef' 'lone. Sometime I put 'em with 'nother lady and wuk. I wuks some with other ladies, some with Gawge. Then I wuks in other field than him, pickin' like beans while he pick 'matoes.

Can you remember where you went from Carolina [to Mr. Smith]?

Les' see. I guess mebbe that must be Ca'lina again [North Carolina?]. There we had good luck 'cause we heerd 'bout needin' lotsa peeples at some cabbage places. So we drives up and there a big sign and we lines up and both gets wuk, 'bout ten day, I think. The childs stays wid a lady in her house and we pays forty-five cents each day. Cabbages is heavy and kinda hard 'cuz they has to be cut and is mos'ly big. But we get 'long and when we leaves we is 'bout even on money; we had 'nuff to go on. Peoples tells us where they's wuk. This time we wuks only two-three day.

Next we gets in de otto and on to quite a long trip and we crosses a big bridge which costest lot and take all money we has. [Four dollars for car and driver and 85 cents for each passenger, a total of $6.55. This is the new seventeen-and-a-half-mile-long Chesapeake Bridge-Tunnel in Virginia. It is located on the chief route (U.S. 13) taken by migrants going north, and is about halfway between Florida and Maine. It is also the main place where statistics are gathered on the Atlantic Coast Stream work force. A federal Farm Labor Information Station located at the Southern approach is open from April 15 to August 15, and offers information to both crew leaders and freewheelers. The Smiths were helped by the office, as Mrs. Smith says.]

(Mrs. Smith): Before we go on the bridge, men talk and say do we need help. Gawge smile and say, "Lawd bless you. We shure does," an' he look up stuff, bring out a map and say, "Go fust to dis-yere place I mark and show this piece paper and you find he need you and give you wuk."

This be in beans 'gain, but we wuks steady [perhaps Virginia or Delaware?]. They is ladies to kere for the childs. This the bes' place for pay an' livin'. They be row and row of bean plant fer mile and mile an' we goes up and down an' pick an' pick. This money give us 'nuff keep us in our trubbles after.

After dat we goes nawth still [Delaware or New Jersey?] but the luck no good for reg'lar wuk. Farmers have many peepuls travel togedder [crews] an' there no place for 'lone peepuls like we's. So for three-four week we drive otto roun' an' roun' and only wuk little at time. We does little 'spargus, which is hard, wid a knife an' lotsa leanin' ovuh. Three day we do 'matoes.

(Mrs. Smith): Once Gawge say, "Le's go back home. We is beat like las' year." (He decourage.) I say, "Le's go on New Yawk." (Some peepuls say there apple and fruit.) I say, "Mebbe things be better then." But he say, "No, we start back. The gas too much awreddy." This be in hot, rainy August, and we not fin' wuk 'lessen wedder be good. So we starts back and here we is.

How we find these-here beans? A man say they be here an' we find wuk. Res' not so good, livin' terrible, an' childs not well. Marie get runs [diarrhea] and quite sick so I keres for her 'stead go in field. But leastwise we now has some money—see? [She shows crumbled bills, mostly of one dollar.] They's moah hid-like.

What will you do now? [This was in mid-September.]

Well, we hits de road back to home, I guess. Mebbe we finds wuk, man say they peanuts on way. [This is probably Suffolk County in southeastern Virginia, where Planters, the largest producers in the country, have vast fields. The crop is harvested from mid-September through November, hence there was a possibility of a considerable period of work for the Smiths.] We done lotsa peanuts betimes in Gawgia. [Georgia peanuts, locally called goobers, are famous, and their oil is widely used in salad oil and margarine.] If we finds wuk there we get home wid good money, and everythin' be all right.

Please answer some special questions about your life on the road [to Mrs. Smith].

What about your living and eating?

This is two ways: sometime we stays in houses, sometime we sleep in de otto. The houses bad, but what to do? They is dirty and crowded. Lotsa peepuls togedder, bad water, and smells.

Toilets? We has buckets to use. Beds? Bad spring or no spring, jes' cot. Bugs? Mos" alway. We gets use to 'em. Not try

to kill cuz dey comes back all time. Cooking? They's stoves, but they bad mos'ly. Light? One 'lectric [bulb] hang from top. Food? We makes do 'n we has learn' what fill de stummick. We buys 'long de way. Nuthin' speshul. Eat what we pickin'.
    When we sleeps in de otto? We is alway tired, so it be easy, and it save money. We has blanket and bedcloses wid us. We puts on seats and floors. Childs on floors, us on seats. We crouches up cuz they not 'nuff room to stretch. It save money. How often? Oh, guess 'bout half de time.

Do you have anything to do with people in the towns you visit?

No, nuthin'. We not look very 'spectable an' we can't keep clean, leastwise not all time. Coupla time we bad off and we find the 'leef peepul, but they do nuthin' cuz they not have no money for furriners [non-residents] like us. But a nice lady give us some money personal and it help us out 'til we wuks 'gain. Oh, yes, one time Claude ak funny, all quiet an' real pale an' sickly, and our boss [farmer] tell us go to place in town and there some nice peepul, a doctor and nuss, get him well. He stay dere all time we wuk and does not aks us fo' no money. They is parties sometime but we nevuh goes 'cause we don' look right and not know how to ak. They is peepul we meet who is real nice and they help us 'long. They is many good peepul in dis worl'.

Do you think you will take this trip next year [to Mr. Smith]?

Well, can't say 'zackly. This trip have some bad luck, but we take home more than las' time. De man at de big bridge stop tell us he see 'bout go wid udders, he tell how we do it. He take name and 'dress and mebbe I get letter tell where go and see man take kere us. So mebbe we not be 'lone. But, yes, we go 'gain. They really nuthin' to home summer 'cep hot. Each two time we learn an' have some bad and some good. It good for see new place an' do new thing. Yes, we prob'ly go 'gain.

What George was trying to say is best expressed in the words of a Negro migrant in Suffolk County, Long Island, New York, quoted in 1967 by a reporter for the *Suffolk*

Sun: "Each year I keep telling myself, 'this is the last time.' But each year I'm back. I don't know why. . . . I guess I'm just pretty easy to convince and I don't know no other life. It's like a disease."

A Snap-Bean Picker

Mrs. Louise Jones (her real name) might be called a professional migrant since, at forty-eight years of age, she is a veteran of the Atlantic Coast Stream. A Negress, she has worked for the same crew leader (also Negro) for eleven annual trips which she has thoroughly enjoyed.

Unlike many others in the Stream, she has been rather remarkably successful. She is therefore far from average, and her experience is a welcome relief from the deplorable conditions which most migrant workers meet.

Mrs. Jones is, in fact, in every way an exceptional woman. Only lack of education has prevented her from becoming a white-collar worker, even a teacher. A combination of circumstances, about which she remains philosophical and uncomplaining, has prevented her from breaking away from the bondage of common labor. Her happy disposition and her acceptance of the life in which she has found herself mark her as an unusual person when compared with her fellow workers in the Stream.

She was interviewed in mid-September, 1967, at Bridgeton, in southern New Jersey (in the county next to where the Lees were picking tomatoes and living under outrageous conditions). She had been on the move since mid-May. In spite of regular work, with only the weekends and the short breaks while traveling to the next contract assignment, she was seemingly fresh. She explained her condition in these words: "Well, I figure there's no need to expect trouble lest it comes. If it comes, it will soon go. It doesn't pay to fret and complain, and if you learn to take things as they are, the Lord gives you strength to go on. If I have a secret, it is that. He never lets me down. It is not meant that I be miserable, and I am not."

As a result, one is not surprised at the complimentary opinion expressed by her crew leader, Amos, under whom she has worked for eleven trips. "Louise Jones," he says, "is an absolute prize in every way, and I can't say enough good things about her. That is why I am sending you to her, because you should have a little happiness in your book. She is also worth half a dozen other workers, a simply grand worker, probably the best of the three thousand I have brought up north these many years [fifteen]."

Mrs. Jones' speech is entirely free of dialect. In spite of the fact that her formal education ceased after two years of high school, she says, "I was always wanting to make a good appearance and impression, and my mother encouraged me to study and watch the manners and speech of the white people she cooked for. I helped out, and when I served a company meal I would listen to everyone and then I practiced myself with a good dictionary. I kept a notebook with words I could use. One of my best teachers had told me to do that."

Needless to say, she proved a very communicative subject, and only the highlights of the interview are reproduced here.

Tell me something about yourself.

I am certainly one of the very luckiest of any Negroes. My parents lived in Augusta, Georgia, when I was born so many years ago. My father owned a small store in the Negro section of town and my mother worked as a "live-out" (that means she came home at nights) cook. The people she worked for were the kind of whites who treated the Negroes so well that we felt like part of the family. I suppose some of the slaves felt the same way.

Anyway, my parents saw that I went to school, which I did until my father was killed by a drunk customer when I was just finishing my second year of high school. With his insurance my mother began to pay on a nice little house, which I later finished paying for. That is why I stopped school, because I had to help my mother by taking care of my three younger brothers and sisters.

Mother never remarried, and even when the family grew up I was still working to help them along—two went to college, Tuskegee Institute, which was very unusual in those days. I took care of my mother for twelve years after she stopped working, and I was in my early thirties when she died. Shortly after, I married Paul Jones, a fine man and a widower, but he passed on after less than a year and a half, and I was on my own.

I continued working, but moved to Florida and bought a little house with the money my Augusta house brought. My aunt came to live with me. That was when I became a field worker. I began working during the Florida harvests. In between times I was still a maid or housekeeper. There is always that kind of work available.

How did you happen to start traveling?

A little more than twelve years ago, my name was given to Amos, who was signing up crew members of bean pickers for his annual trip north. He convinced me that I should go along at least once, as he was experienced and he contracted with only the finest and fairest, best-pay bean growers. He worked day-haul in my area during the winter season, and used the same buses and trucks for the northern trip.

Since I could still continue my picking and household work for six or more months, it sounded right good to me. I had been working in tomatoes, celery, and asparagus as well as beans, both pole and snap. I liked beans best, so I agreed to try. He explained everything so there would be no surprises. On this first trip, eleven years ago, there were over a hundred workers (and about sixty wives and children) and we went in four buses and a truck, all going together. Well, this trip was o.k. for me. I brought back about four hundred and fifty dollars (and this was when money meant more than it does now).

What about this present trip?

Well, I have followed almost the same route and gone to the same places each year, except a couple of farms where they use machines now instead of us. Amos just found other places to keep us busy; that is one good thing about him. He makes it possible to work as much as we want, and it is nice and homey to go to the same places and meet the same people and work in the same fields. We know what to expect, and there is no trouble about food and shelter. As a matter of fact, I have stayed in exactly the same houses in several camps for about seven or eight years, and it just seems as if I am right at home.

This year we have so far been in four states, only with snap beans. We do nothing else, except some of the men do weeding and hoeing on the plants not yet ready to pick. The harvests seem to work out just right, as Amos and the farmers planned. This year, because of the heavy rains everywhere, the beans were ready early, and therefore we knew in advance not to go where it had been finished. But Amos found other places that needed us. It is funny, but sometimes the harvest time is different within fifty or a hundred miles!

This is our present trip [*she consults my crop map*]:

>   May 15–June 15: South Carolina. Eastern Shore, not far
>   from Charleston.
>   June 20–July 15: Delaware.
>   July 17–mid-August: Maryland. Eastern Shore.
>   August 17–(I think it was)–September 15: Southern New
>   Jersey, Bridgeton. [Interview took place here.]
>   Future:
>   September 17–November 10 (approximate): Again in
>   Maryland, Eastern Shore, for late crops.

We will then go direct to Florida, dropping off some people along the way who live north of Florida or in other southern states (they may have been hired in Florida or in their home states and joined us).

In every crew there are lots of beginners along the first time, but many have been along for almost as long as I have. The average? I guess about four or five years. You see, we work at a piece rate and us experienced workers can pick about five hundred to six hundred pounds a day. The slower ones, I should say, about half as much. We get two cents a pound. I average about twelve dollars a day, but remember, I work five days a week and have to pay five dollars a week for my room plus my food. We also spend at least two-three days between jobs. Last year I took back about eleven hundred dollars; this year it may be over that. Lots of the workers, especially with families, take home very little because they take days off, are sick, and don't save their money. Families, of course, are more expensive to keep.

Hand bean-picking is hard. We are not exactly stoop labor; it is much easier to move along the rows on our knees (some have housemaid's knee [*laughs*]). To protect our knees we wear big, thick pads. We have baskets; when they are full, field hands bring us empty ones, give us a ticket, and take the full ones to be loaded on trucks. So we don't have to carry heavy loads since we only move our baskets along with us.

We experienced pickers have learned to pick only the best beans, the ones fully ripe and ready, and we are careful to separate any dirt or leaves. Some plants will have other beans ripe a little later; sometimes we go back through the rows, sometimes later pickers do.

Being paid by the amount, not by the hour, makes us work steady. We stop at noon for some sandwiches and a cold drink or coffee, which we buy and eat wherever we are. Some of the farmers have water at various places, and toilets, too (these are chemical), so we do not have to go far.

At the end of the day the buses pick us up and take us back to the camp.

How about your living conditions?

Very fine, as I told you. Most of our places are cement (some wood) and I share a room with a friend. We each have our own bed, and there is a gas stove and a sink with running water. The toilet is a little way off. We always have a window or two, and one light hanging from the ceiling. The whole building is divided into these rooms, with a center aisle.

We are very happy in our camps because some I have heard of are quite awful. But the best farmers seem to feel it is worth making the workers happy.

Do you have anything to do with the people in the towns you visit?

Goodness, yes, that is one of the reasons I look forward to these trips. From what I hear, I guess we are lucky. On weekends we have movies, shows, fun nights, and parties and dances. The white people are so nice, and it is fine to know they have been thinking and planning for us.

For those with children, it is always a problem what to do with them if the mother wants to work in the fields. They cannot be left on their own, especially the younger ones, and Amos will not let the older ones—I mean below about fifteen —work for fear of losing his license, because of the laws. So these children have to be taken care of. Some towns have nice places to keep the children [day care] and places to play and get out of doors, and even some classes. Also there are health places for examinations and to get medicines.

Mostly I know about how nice it is to watch the workers have a good time. Amos runs one or two of his buses in to town, so everyone has a chance to go if they want to, even to the stores. It is much like home.

What do you think of Amos?

Well, you know how we both feel about each other. He seems to know exactly what to do and how to keep us happy. He is always in the fields when we are. He knows all the rules. Having worked with almost the same farmers for such a long time, they play fair with him. His wife is along (their children are grown and on their own) and she takes an interest in the womenfolk. [And much more of this kind of complimentary comment.]

Will you be back next year?

Of course. Absolutely. Probably I will want to be less active before too long and I will probably give up these trips, but still work picking in Florida. Then one day I would only do day housework, and maybe at last rest all the time.

But for now I will be back next year and maybe several more years as long as I am happy.

A "Single" Potato Harvester

William (Bill) Allen, a twenty-nine-year-old white man from Florida, characterizes himself as a "loner," since for four years he has been "on the loose," without any family ties. In the vocabulary of migrant labor he is a "single," that is, he travels without a family and in a crew of other singles, most of whom are much older and, in his case, less reliable. However, singles are often preferred to families by many growers for the understandable reason that housing is less of a problem and that such men are free of the obligations associated with marriage and children.

A ruggedly handsome and muscular man, Bill would be noticed anywhere and recognized as a physical worker. His face is well-proportioned, his eyes clear, and his expression open, showing little of the inner bitterness he reveals in conversation. The first impression he communicates is one of arrogance and self-sufficiency, but behind this façade obviously lies a complicated, insecure person.

Bill has now been a loner for enough time to have settled into a way of life apparently satisfactory to him, particularly in the freedom from responsibility, which he enjoys.

His white crew leader, Joe, likes Bill and is satisfied with both his attitude and his work. "Bill is a little out of the ordinary, you know," he says, "and once you have learned to understand what makes him tick (which I believe I do after four years with him), you find many good qualities which make him far above the average of his fellow-workers who, as a rule, are certainly a mixed lot. In such groups, which I have been organizing now for about a dozen years, a truly good, responsible man is quite rare. Bill is such a man. Such weaknesses as he has are personal and do not interfere with his work.

"I suggested him because you should have in your book a single who is not like the rest. The bad ones, the troublemakers for everyone involved, are all too numerous in this business, but then, they would not be on the season if they were otherwise than they are—a rough lot, but hard workers because they want but one thing, the money. What they do with it is their own business, certainly none of mine. What I am paid for and interested in is only that they produce. Long since I have learned not to meddle in their off-the-job behavior, which has given a black eye to the good migrant workers, who are the majority. I keep them under control in their work; that is my only responsibility to the growers, their employers, as I see it.

"You could talk for hours with these bums about themselves and their work, but you would not really know them because they would tell you fantastic stories, completely untrue, about themselves, and they would feed you lots of false information and would boast of things they never accomplished. Either that, or they would go all out in griping and giving a false impression of their work and me, their crew leader. Most of them are mixed-up hellers who would just love to get into a book in a spectacular, shocking way, as if to justify their wasted personal lives.

"Bill, however, is different, completely different, and decent as well, which is a miracle in view of his companions."

At the time of taping, in August, 1967, Bill's crew of potato harvesters had advanced north as far as the Eastern Shore of Maryland (near Hurlock) and were yet to work an additional two months in Delaware and Suffolk County, Long Island, New York.

Here, then, is Bill Allen.

Tell me about yourself and your life before you became a migrant worker.

I am originally from a small town in Iowa, a helluva place to be born and to live in. Of course I was a farm boy, else why would I be doing what I am? I guess that old saw about being close to the soil is about right, because I always did like growing things. I liked to help in planting, in cultivating, and in harvesting; it was a good feeling.

I was my father's right-hand "man," I guess you would call it [*laughs*] even as a boy. He depended on me rather than the full-time hired man from the time I started heavy work, when I was twelve. I was always strong and proud of my physique even when I was not yet fully developed. Later on someone told me I was a narcissist, though I didn't even know the meaning of the word. My mother and father were always proud of me and the way I worked and, yes, I was spoiled, dirt-spoiled.

My life 'til I was sixteen was all school and work. I followed the usual life pattern of a farm boy—up at dawn, chores, off to school, a full school day, home again, more chores, all that bit. When there was special work I just stayed home from school, since I didn't like it much. It wasn't the teacher's fault, I just couldn't see the point (that's why I understand these dropouts, the fools; to be something, you have to have schooling, that I have learned). But my folks didn't care about my grades, and I just wanted to please them (they should see me now!).

As I said, I liked the farm, mainly because I didn't know anything else. I began to get uneasy and dissatisfied in my early teens. I didn't know why—I never seem to know the "why" of things even now. Well, I was always a great reader, and

I got big ideas about going out into the world—it was my oyster, I thought, with all the best out there just waiting for me to grab it. When I was nearly seventeen I did something very decisive—I ran away from those nice people, my folks, and that wonderful life. (At least it seems that way now, looking back.) I had saved some money and I just took off one day. It was almost impulsive (or compulsive), and I'm damned if I can explain it even now. Oh, I have a guilt feeling about it still, I guess.

I was big for my age, so I could easily pass for eighteen, which I did when I enlisted in the Marines in Des Moines, my first stop. Why? You tell me; I guess it was that idea of being rough and tough and glamorous in the blues and reds of the uniform. And, of course, you could prove yourself, and I had always been accepted and overloved (is there such a word? If not, let's say "smothered"), and I had an idea I would be able to accomplish something on my own.

I sure did. During my two-year enlistment (I finally became a sergeant, just like in the movies), I went to training and schools and traveled around—the usual military bit—and let me tell you, I *was* something, to myself, at least [*laughs*].

Well, just about the time my enlistment period was up, I made my second mistake. I was only nineteen, but twenty on the books. I met a girl in Washington—I was at Quantico, the big Marine station—and, you guessed it, I fell in love. She was a secretary, and she didn't like the military life, what she knew of it, and that was very little. She had an idea, very fixed and stubborn, that it would take years to be tops in the Marines. She didn't want to wait; she wanted the honeymoon cottage, maids, cars, and all that right away. I will say she was very young and I was very young and, well, in fear of losing her I made my third mistake (boo-boos are always very clear when one looks back): I did not reenlist and I left the service. That's what love does!

Well, I had some money saved—I have always been a saver —quite a considerable amount, so we decided to marry right away and start life together in that dream world which is called sunny Florida. You know that bit—a wonderful life, free of care, in the sunshine. We settled near Orlando in the center part of the state, and I worked in citrus—orange and lemons—as a work supervisor in a big plant, which shall be nameless. I was considered "too bright" to waste as a common laborer and there's the rub. I was still a farm boy at heart, and I should have been out in the groves, but the pay was better supervising in the packinghouse and my wife did not want me to be a "dirty, common" worker. I got along well, but—here we go again—it wasn't satisfying.

We had a nice house, lots of friends, and right on the dot I became a father. It was a girl; why I was disappointed I didn't know, but I was. Of course now (again the backward glance) I know I wanted my own image in a son. And after that my wife seemed to center her life around Dorothy, the baby. I was out, or at least put in second place. Then we had another girl, Amy, which was even harder for me to take. Call me a fool, because that's what I was, but when Dorothy was almost three I got fed up with getting no attention, playing house and second fiddle. Another mistake—there seem to be lots of them with me—I separated from my wife. It was friendly, even though she could not understand it. My explanation was that I needed my freedom to be myself, not tied down. I agreed to a support deal and lit out.

So eager was I to be free that I disappeared, as far as she was concerned. I took this name; it is not my own, which I will not tell you. I went to another part of Florida and cultivated and picked oranges; this was what I wanted at the time. But I never turned back, and here I am. That tape will run out long before we get to what you want to hear. This is all preliminary. Next question!

How did you happen to become a wandering worker?

You should see it without my telling you: to cover up my failure and rashness. Every single in this crew would have some such tale to tell. Maybe they make it up, but it's all the same. Most of them have been married, the marriage was a disappointment, whether or not they admitted it was their fault. Some punish themselves by drinking and raising hell, but we are all brothers as far as our backgrounds are concerned.

Well, after a year in the groves, I heard of a man who needed about forty willing-to-work guys to go north to harvest potatoes. Our way would be paid, we would travel in a bus he owned, and he would schedule a full work season with good pay. We would bunk together, eat together, and work together. This man was Joe, an old hand as a crew chief, and as good a guy as I have ever met. Well, I really was lonely and that old wandering feeling—you called us wandering workers—got me again. I no longer had any contact with my wife and I figured she could get rid of me on the basis of desertion under the "Enoch Arden" law, which means if a husband wasn't heard of for a certain number of years the wife could sue for an "absent" divorce. I guess I began to be too ashamed to face up to the problem.

So I joined up with Joe, and this is my fourth season. In between I go back to Florida in the bus and work in citrus until it is time to start again, generally in the middle of May. Oh, yes, I should tell you that I send cash to my wife quite regularly, but I have Joe address the envelope and mail it at some town between our places of work.

Tell me about this trip.

It is almost exactly the same route as the other three trips, since Joe signs contracts with the same growers in the same places. He gets the work from the men, and that is really an achievement with us bums [*laughs*]. However, we are, I must say, good workers, and they are hard to find.

This is where we have been and where we will go from here [Maryland]:

>   May, last two weeks: Beaufort, South Carolina, near Charleston and the coast.
>   June 3–July 3: New Bern and Washington, North Carolina. Time between three growers.
>   July 6–31: Norfolk, Virginia, Eastern Shore.
>   August 1–20: Hurlock, Maryland, Eastern Shore. [Interview took place here.]
>   Future schedule:

August 25–September 5 (approximate): Dover and Preston, Delaware, Eastern Shore.
September 10–October 20 (approximate, depending on mechanization, which is increasing): Suffolk County, eastern Long Island, New York.

Then back to Florida in a three- or four-day trip. Citrus work in Florida, his base, is continuous, though Bill stays clear of central Florida and his wife, who he believes is still in Orlando, on the assumption that the cash he has sent has been received by her.

If she is not there or not located, the postoffice can have it; I see they have a continuous deficit, and maybe this will help [*laughs*]. Anyway, my conscience is clear, since I sent it.

Our crew is naturally close together all the time. Some are old timers like me, some have been on all four trips, but there are always about two-thirds new faces. They seem to come and go.

The main white-potato producers are far in the north, you know, and they use the newly developed diggers almost completely. Most of the southeastern and eastern states don't have mechanical harvesters, which makes it ideal for me.

Do you know the process of hand-harvesting? Before we arrive, a mechanical digger has uprooted the potatoes and left them to be picked up. The vines or plants are very often still attached. We go along the rows and pick up the potatoes from the ground, separating them from the plants and attached soil or weeds. We carry sacks which, as you can imagine, get very heavy as they are filled. That's why there is no place for a weakling in this work.

We put the filled sacks along the rows where they are picked up and loaded into trucks (by the men who are called "buckers" in the business). We do not do any hand-sorting (by size) except when the crop is all picked and we are still around.

Picking is hard work; I guess you have heard of stoop labor. Moving the heavy bags along the rows uses our shoulder muscles, too; that's why we are all so well developed above the waist as well as in the thighs. [He makes a face like a weight lifter and stands with his chest puffed out and his biceps flexed as in physical culture magazine photographs, laughing as he does so]. Feel these muscles, they're hard as rocks. You could hit me hard and I wouldn't feel anything. It is the hardest kind of work, but we all have good constitutions and good health. If we didn't, Joe would bounce us pronto. The sorting is done in the warehouse, and they usually have special people for that.

Do I get tired? I sure do, but I sleep well.

We are paid by the piece-rate (bag), the amount we can pick, which can go as high as $2.50 an hour, though the average, with mixed sizes, is more like $1.85 or two dollars. Working five days a week, eight to ten hours a day, we certainly make good money in comparison with other field workers.

Most growers have water at the ends of the rows, as well as portable toilets. Joe, who is always around to supervise us, gives us breaks every hour; he insists on that. A good man, that Joe.

What do you think of your crew leader?

You talked to Joe, and he introduced you to me. He knows what I think of him. He is the best as far as I am concerned.

Joe has an almost impossible job in trying to keep this bunch happy and working, and he does what I call a superior job. Most of the singles are already independent, and they are on the loose, running away from something. Of the forty-odd I would say that only about ten were really reliable and steady; the rest you never know about, but he handles them with kid gloves most of the time. They are really like a lot of children; you never know what their moods will be or what they might do. His method to keep them under control is a combination of force, physical and mental, and a certain sort of diplomacy combined with patience. What patience that guy has! He puts up with everything until he reaches a near breaking point.

He holds a strong rein because he is a leader who never lets things get out of control. Outwardly he is tough, but I and a few others know he is soft as jelly. This talk of discipline sounds bad, but he has found it is the only way. If he let things get out of hand just once, he would be lost. It is kind of like my officers in the Marines. We knew they meant business, but as long as they were always fair and patient we did not mind. The trick with Joe is that he keeps his cool—you know that expression? Actually, these men look for discipline, and respect him for his control.

When we sign up with him, before we start out, he puts it on the line what he wants and what he expects so that there will never be any kickback or excuses. He knows that to let up even a little would lead to their taking advantage of him and then he would lose control. One way he works his will is to never let them forget he is the boss, and he will not put up with any monkey business in the fields. He works it in such a way that they would feel ashamed and disloyal if their actions caused trouble for him. He would not hesitate a minute to fire someone—he has done it a few times—and leave him stranded far from the south home base.

You will not be surprised to know that he curses something awful; this is about the only way to show his displeasure, and it keeps them in line. Of course, they gripe a lot and call him "Hitler" and "dictator" and other less complimentary names. If one hates him for a while, it soon changes when he calms down.

The main trouble he has with us is over drinking, mostly cheap wine, and brawling. The first is a part of being lonely, I guess, the second more or less natural with so many individuals traveling, living, and working together. In regard to the drinking, it is only on nonworking weekends for the most part, for they know the troubles in working as hard as they do with a hangover. He never lets anyone work (and they lose the pay, naturally) if the aftereffects show. The fighting he ignores as long as it is not general. He figures that they need to let off steam.

Joe does almost everything a crew leader, as I understand it, should. He is registered as required, has insurance for both the bus and the workers, keeps payroll records, and acts as a mother confessor to his crew members. If a vote was to be taken, he would rate very high, I am sure.

What about your life as a migrant?

The key to my life is to find what happiness I can. I believe I have learned to do that. Several mistakes I have not made. First, I have not gotten too close to the others; I have only one or two real friends besides Joe (some say I make up to him too much). I don't ever take sides in the feuds and fights. I am really an observer of what is around me. I mind my own business, do my work well (Joe will tell you that), and that's that.

Living so close together is hard on a person like me. First of all, there is no privacy. You can get away from the noise and hubbub, you can be apart from everything, even though that does not make for popularity. Most of them think I am snooty and feel superior to them; well, I do. I am a fiend for cleanliness—showers are the first thing I look for. I try to get a cot or bunk in a corner, and I am not particular about the mattress because I sleep well and am used to the noise and movement as a part of the life. In general, our dormitories have up to eighty or more men, our crew and another, and eighty or ninety men cooped up can make lots of trouble and noise, especially since they are all different individuals.

The chief indoor sport seems to be gambling, to which I have no objection. If a fellow wants to waste his hard-earned money, that is his affair, not mine. I happen to dislike card games.

What do I like? Well, reading. I have always liked books, and these paperbacks are a lifesaver. I am always in the middle of two or three at once. I make deals with public libraries to leave a hefty deposit so I can take books out. I have never failed to return them before I leave the place. Give me a good book and I am happy. There are not many people to really talk with, I mean true talk, so I have the books.

A very good thing about me is that I am responsible. Any grower who pays me deserves the best, and I for one give it to him. Besides, output determines pay, and that I want. What do I do with my money? I save it for spending when I am back in Florida. I have good clothes and I have a very nice room there, and I date and stuff. I am saving for maybe my own grove somewhere. Then and only then will I leave this potato bit.

We eat together, and Joe sees to it that we have good food, for which we pay. We pay an average of six dollars weekly for the bunking.

How much will I make from this trip? Well, last year I had one thousand four hundred dollars when I got back home. It went into the bank. Potato specialists can make good money, good compared to other pay in harvesting, if they work regularly and produce well. It all depends. For me it is better than straight salary or the hour rate. Some of the crew get back with practically nothing. We drop some off along the way, and you would be surprised—or would you?—at how broke they are. All that work and time for nothing.

Will you be taking this trip next year?

Absolutely. You see, I have this objective and therefore a purpose, I guess you would call me a "pro." Eventually I will settle down (or will I?) [*laughs sardonically*]. Who knows? I figure I am still young and footloose, and I will follow my life pattern just so long as I am fairly happy, which I am right now. This suits me swell.

3

On the Season: The Central Stream

The Texicans (Mexican-Americans) following the four substreams (Appendix III) of the Central Stream form the largest number of the total American migrant interstate farm workers because of the large number who also work in the Pacific Coast Stream, but the approximately 135,000 in the Central Stream, 90 percent of the total, make it the largest of the three.

Furthermore, the Mexican-Americans, with their generally large families, do not like to leave any of their children, of whatever age, at home. This stream therefore might well be termed "the family stream." The crew buses and trucks—more trucks are used for transportation than in the other streams—are filled to overflowing with children, ranging from infants to teen-agers. Unless forbidden when the child labor laws are enforced, most of the children ten and above work in the fields with their parents. There always seems to be a girl below ten or twelve who cares for those still younger while the mother is absent at work. Or when several children work, the mother may remain in camp with the younger children and babies. Because of family size, adequate housing is a problem, though the Texicans rarely complain when three or four children, often both boys and girls together, must sleep in the same bed. Nor do the parents object to sharing their bed with babies and/or younger children.

The Texicans are basically happy people, outwardly appearing to adjust to any discomfort. They are, however, intensely emotional and given to moods of unhappiness, even despair. For this reason crew leaders like José Montero (Chapter 6) tend to treat them like children. (Crew leaders in all the streams maintain a "father image" in varying degrees.) The recognition of the leader as the boss is continuously reflected in their referring to him as *"el patron"* (the boss) rather than by his first name or "Mister."

Their speech is interspersed with many equivalent Spanish words or phrases when they are unable to summon up English words and terms.

Las Fresas y Los Pepinos (Strawberries and Cucumbers), East Branch

Though he appears much older because his sun-worn face is like tough leather, Rodrigo Sanchez admits to forty years. He, his wife, Chiquita, and their three children— Carlos, fifteen; Clarita, twelve; and Juan, eight—live in northeast Texas very near the Oklahoma border. It is not a town, he declares, only a collection of shacks, with a small store, a gas station, and nothing else. The nearest town is nine miles away; it is very *grande* (big). [The latest census enumerates a little over four thousand population!]

During the winter he works in various crops as a day-haul laborer. His specialty there is cotton, and he is a chopper; machines do the picking. He is employed more or less regularly; he is never rich, he says, but he is able to *hacer* (to make out).

The children attend school—the trip is twelve miles each way—only from November to mid-April, when the annual northern journey begins. But because of the long distance, twelve miles each way, they have to leave their mother alone, and Rodrigo believes this is not good. There is nothing unusual about his house, Rodrigo says; it is of unpainted wood, with four rooms and two porches, front and back, but he proudly announces that it is always *limpia* (clean) and gives full credit to his wife. Their life is apparently unexciting; the best part, in fact the highlight, of the year is when they take *el viaje largo* [the long trip], because that is when they are together all the time.

Rodrigo was born in Texas near the Rio Grande River, so he is a proud *Norteamericano*. He is able to "make sentences" in English because he went to school until he was eleven. Like most of the Mexican-Americans in the Central Stream, the family is monolingual, preferring Spanish to their smattering of English. Much of the interview was interrupted by Carlos, who was very proud of his activities as interpreter. Rodrigo was not given to volubility; he was ill at ease and more than slightly suspicious, particularly since what he said was to be in a book. Carlos promised to read *la letra* (the words) to him. Carlos also insisted that he listen to a rerun of the tape so that he would hear *la verdad* (the truth).

The October interview took place in a southern Illinois migrant camp, where the Sanchez family were picking fall apples. This was the last stop before their return to Texas after six months away from home.

How did you happen to start these yearly trips?

Very simple. Lots of people of our race in Texas take the journey. I decided to start out ten years ago, when a man with a truck came by while I was working in the cotton and told me I could make good money if I went north. Chiquita did not want to stay alone at home, so four months later we started out. The truck carried thirty-five people and we rode on piles of mattresses which we took into the houses where we stayed, because the first thing we found out was that the springs on the beds we could feel through the blankets which covered them. Sometimes we four—Carlos was five and Clarita two— slept in one big bed. Other times we had two beds, but we always used the mattresses we carried with us.

Only my wife and I worked; I forget what we picked except that it was hard work, and we were always tired. That first trip we went as far as Michigan, where we did sugar beets for six weeks. But since the driver paid for near everything, we went home with I think it was three hundred dollars, which was a lot of money. It was worthwhile, so we just started out every year with the same man. *El patron* (the crew leader, chief) was jolly and was fair with us, so we have been with him ever since. He bought a new truck five years ago, and we did not have any troubles on the road except for some flat tires and once in a while stops for repairs which he made himself since he works as a mechanic in Texas.

We are all happy by nature, we sleep and we sing and there is always a *muchacho* who plays a guitar, and we do not mind the bouncy trip at all. As the childrens grew up, we left them at home with a cousin some years to go to school. Chiquita missed one trip when Juan was born, and I did not see him until he was half a year old! She went on the next trip with the baby and from that year on she always work with me. Sometimes the childrens stay at the ends of the rows so she could look after them whenever she get back to that part. Sometimes we left them in the cabin with Carlos to watch them. He was always a good baby-sitter [Carlos beams] and he took good care of them. My son is *una buena madre* [a good mother]!

We have pick all kinds of thing: of vegetables—asparagus,

tomatoes, onions, sugar beets, peas, cucumbers, and strawberries; of fruits—cherries, apples, and peaches. For last four
years we do only strawberries and cucumbers. *El patron* always
fix it that we are *los especialistas* [specialists]. This is that we
are fast and we know what ready to pick and what wait.

Tell me about this trip.

Like most other. Same peoples go ever year, they our friends
now and all from same part of Texas. We do only same things,
except now apples. [He consults a small notebook in which
he records expenses, wages and other information; it is his
log book.]

El patron come get us in middle April. We go in two days to
Arkansas, next door, and works for four weeks. [May is the
peak season in Arkansas, when four times the usual number
of migrants are employed; they are en route to the north.] The
camp she very good with showers—only in few places so good
—and we eat outdoor on big table, all together. Strawberries not
always big and red at same time, and we go back to same fields
to pick same plants until they is none left.

Strawberries is *mas bonitas* [the prettiest] of all; they is all
kinds of nice red and all sizes. The big ones is pretty enough
to paint. Funny, the children do not like them because of the
little seeds. When they be for stores we pick with stems on
and we is careful keep good stems and not crush so they will
look nice in boxes. We does not put them in little boxes; there
is a place where peoples put them by sizes. When they be for
freezing we no care because they is sliced later and is never
whole. Carlos always picks, Clarita sometimes. We is paid by
the box. [But he is unable to say how much.]

Then one day we drive on for two days to near where we
are now [southern Illinois]. We stay at same big farm for
two week. Again it is strawberries. We never tired of strawberries—Chiquita say we *smell* strawberries and our fingers is
red from juice. Carlos work only little because of laws. [He
is underage under the federal law.]

Next we travels to Wisconsin and it is long stay [from June
16 to September 30]. We are in middle of state [in Waushara
County]. For first month we again pick strawberries, and are

real at home. [By far the largest number of migrant workers in Wisconsin are from Texas, almost eight thousand (82 percent) in 1964.] They ask us pick cherries, not enough workers, but *el patron* say *"No."* We good at strawberries and we stay until done.

But for longest time we do cucumbers. They is [used] for pickles. The factories [processing plants] is right near and we learns right away what to pick. We works from sunup to sundown, and we is paid by size; they is several pickings base[d] on ripe[ness], but finally we cleans out the rows.

Pay? This was best of all; *el patron* has good deal. We each gets 'bout five dollar day. The farmer not pay, but company [processor] do, right at end of day, so we know what we make. This different from usual, where *el patron* pay us. Also we has the social security. Some works at sorting in factory, but we only picks. *El patron* drives truck to carry what we pick to factory. But he does not have our monies.

Oh, yes, the other special thing is extra money at end [the last week in September]. I no understand the 'rithmetic but it depend on what we picks. [This is a bonus given to those who remain for the full season.] This is best money we made [Rodrigo's bookkeeping is his carefully-guarded secret, so he will not reveal the amount.]

After that we start back home and here we are. *El patron* get us work to pick these apples which is not as hard as strawberries and cucumbers. Two oldest childrens help. We be in Texas in November. First thing Chiquita will buy ice box to keep food nice; she keep the money she earn; it be hers and she decide how spend. The childrens all goes to school. I start work there again.

Tell me something about your life on this trip.

We have *la suerte* [luck]. All houses and camps good, not like all *los cuentos relatos* [the tales]. This is because of *el patron*. Food? *Bueno.* The childrens? Most time they work, but sometime Juan go school [summer classes]. All three has the health examination. Some *padres* [parents] take children to fields every day but they get tired. Some places *el patron* not let them work [the federal or state laws]. But they do their share. The towns? No, we never see the peoples. They is far away 'cept for health and Juan's classes.

What about next year?

Of course we start again just like always. This truck you see is *nuestro hogar* [our home away from home]. We would be *infeliz* [unhappy] without it.

The Sanchez family appears to be somewhat typical of Texicans. The ten trips have united the workers in the crew; they are a family, as it were. Their basic happiness and acceptance of the facts of migrant life have made them reasonably happy on *el viaje largo* (the long trip). Rodrigo expressed this in words approximating the following: "We travel, we work, we eat, we sleep. Why worry? *La vida está difícil* (Life is hard)."

Two Teen-Age Loners on the East Branch

Seventeen-year-old Pancho Rivera (he is nearing his eighteenth birthday) is a veteran of the Mexican-American trek northward from Texas to the Great Lakes. For the past three seasons he has traveled alone, as a "single." He stoutly maintains and wants it definitely understood that he is *not* a *caminata* (hobo or tramp). As if to prove this, he took a roll of bills from his pocket and tossed it nonchalantly from hand to hand to show his financial independence, a gesture which lost some of its intended effect when his companion, eighteen-year-old Hector Gonzalez, another loner, who also participated in the interview, laughingly remarked that the thick wad was of one dollar bills!

Most singles in the various streams travel in buses as crew members; they are not only single men, but also married men traveling without their families. But, experienced in the life on the season, Pancho and Hector are completely self-sufficient; they are on their own and never solicit or need help. In fact, they would seem to resent even the suggestion of dependence. This pride in personal freedom is unusual among migrant harvesters, most of whom need the security of leadership and guidance.

Pancho is a handsome, yellow-brown adolescent, with flashing eyes. Hector, who met Pancho the previous year while both were working in a Michigan cherry orchard, is a somewhat squat, pimple-faced youth leaning to fatness. He is the comedian of the duo; life is outwardly a great deal of fun; worries are few and far between, for Hector gives the impression that nothing will—or can—daunt him. He has worked on the season for three years, and, unlike Pancho, he has always been on his own.

After the 1966 harvests they agreed to meet and work together again in the summer of 1967. During the winter months in Texas they did not keep in touch with each other, though they live less than a hundred miles apart. Each hitchhiked north separately in early May.

Hitchhiking, Pablo explained, is easier when traveling alone; a truck or automobile driver hesitates to pick up a couple for fear of being mugged. Both have learned through experience the "art" of securing free rides, and each has developed a technique of ingratiating himself so that he can remain with the driver as far as he is going. They "operate" so entertainingly and skillfully that lone drivers more frequently than not pay for meals and even let them share motel accommodations from time to time. They have developed, Pancho says, an "act" which is effective in easing their journeys. The main thing, according to Hector, is to be completely honest yet calculating. It never seems to have occurred to either to resort to violence, threats, or theft, perhaps because they know that the highway police of the four states through which they travel to their Michigan destination—Arkansas, Missouri, Illinois, and Indiana—could easily spot them later.

To them, moving on the main highways is both quicker and more comfortable. [They failed to mention that soliciting rides on state roads is against the law.] They both figure that they more than repay a driver by 1) being clean in both body and clothes, 2) carrying on an impersonal conversation, and 3) being either an interesting story-teller or, more often, an attentive listener. "I could write a book about the people who have given me lifts," says Pancho. "They will tell the most personal things, ask your advice on problems they want to talk about to a stranger. All you have to do is to listen and you have won them over."

One rule they have established: they never accept rides from single women or several women in the same car. "Women can cause trouble and delay," they agreed. Pancho learned this the hard way on his first trip, but revealed no details. Families or couples are also undesirable: too many stops and too much of an effort to be pleasant. Similarly, two or three men traveling together are unsatisfactory; "You are an outsider," says Hector.

What was to have been a tape recording with Pancho alone became a joint interview, each adding his bit of information to the story of the other. They had completed four months of work along the shore of Lake Michigan in a concentrated area from Muskegon, Michigan, in the north to Benton Harbor in the south, and were picking tomatoes in northwest Indiana near South Bend when they were interviewed in October. This was their last stop of the 1967 season.

Both Pancho and Hector were unique in that, unlike other Mexican-Americans, they spoke quite good unaccented English, lapsing only occasionally into their native Spanish.

Tell me something about yourself [to Pancho].

Well, I began this life with my family when I was ten years old. We came north—my father, mother, a younger brother, and an older sister—every year as regular as clockwork. We had a 1956 Pontiac which my father kept in top condition—he was a good mechanic—and we carried clothes, bedding, and equipment in the trunk, with other stuff tied on the top. All of us picked, every sort of crop.

At first we stopped many places, one year at ten different farms, but we learned to forget working on the way to Michigan and five years ago started coming directly nonstop. After the season, we returned to Texas. We lived near Tyler, where my father worked winters in a garage. One day, he was killed when a car rolled off a grease-pit elevator and ran over him. My mother stopped traveling, and my sister was married.

I decided to hit the road alone. I was fifteen then, but looked older. I have never had anyone ask any questions about my age, so I just kept my mouth shut and no one seemed to know any different. It has worked well.

I learned the hard way. There was always a job somewhere, and I used to ask around to find where workers were needed, then I would bum a ride to the farm they told me about. Because I was alone I had no housing troubles, though I did stay in some pretty awful places. Sometimes I was in dormitories with a lot of men who traveled together in crews—every kind of man you can imagine.

Over the last three trips I have learned a lot, and by working hard I have taken back some real good money, because a guy alone can work as much as he likes. I have done any and every kind of work—strawberries, cherries, apples, cucumbers, raspberries, peaches, asparagus, tomatoes, blueberries. Each one is a little different, but if you mind your business and work well you can always get along. Though I have not had much education since I was fourteen, I have lots of things going for me which are more important than those in books.

How about this trip [to Pancho and Hector]?

We left Texas about the same time, late in April. We both had winter jobs and did not have to worry about money.

[Hector lives with his family; Pancho, in a rooming house.] But the summer is our good time. There is nothing like being on your own [Pancho]; no responsibilities, just a good life, as good as I can make it [Hector]. The trip took six days, because I stopped over a whole weekend in Illinois with a fellow who had driven me from St. Louis and took me home with him; his wife and kids were fine, and they gave me twenty dollars to help me on my way, since they thought I was hard up! [Pancho]. I traveled in three days almost solid; made the trip with only five hitches, most of them long distance—one was a truck driver who took me over five hundred miles. Pancho does not like trucks, but I don't mind [Hector].

We always plan to meet near Benton Harbor on the shore of Lake Michigan, where we work first for the same farmer, picking asparagus. The first one who arrives saves a bunk for the other in the men's dormitory. Asparagus picking is really killing work and that is why we do it first, for about four weeks in May. This takes a lot of judgment, because not all the spears are ready to be cut at the same time, and several cuttings are necessary. Asparagus takes more time than almost any other vegetable, and that is why we stay so long. This farmer wants us to pick spears of just one approximate size, since the crop is for canning. In bunches for stores it is not necessary to pay as much attention to size because a housewife can paw over the display to find the sizes she likes. Some places used the mechanical harvester for both green and white asparagus, but we use the sharp knife. The stems are supposed to be cut on a bias like cut flowers; this has something to do with staying fresh.

There are two ways of paying: either $1.25 an hour or four cents a pound. A worker can choose one or the other. Since we want to make as much money as possible, we chose the pound rate and came out much better, I think about $1.60 an hour. That is a lot of asparagus! This farmer was very good, and he appreciated quality work. [Unfortunately, seasonal workers in general take little pride in their work; they just seem to want to get it done and be paid.]

We heard that the strawberries not far away were ripening ahead of time because of the hot weather. So we called a farmer and he said to come right away, he could use us both. We picked for two weeks in early June. These were for market, so they had to be picked when they were big. We were paid fifty to sixty cents per eight quarts.

After that we went up north a short way to Muskegon, where we picked blueberries. They are terrible, because each berry is a problem, since it must not be crushed. The pay was $1.35 an hour, which we liked better because if we picked by the quart we would never make much money. The stains were bad, and we had that awful purple under our finger nails for weeks afterward.

Then we went a few miles south to Holland to pick cherries; there is a cherry festival there each year while we are working. We picked from ladders, keeping the stems. We stayed there until about the first of August. Then we picked apples for six weeks, until mid-September. The pay was from a quarter to thirty-five cents a bushel. This was what is called spot picking, which means we picked only ripe fruit. We could pick about nine bushels an hour, so we averaged about two dollars an hour, which isn't bad for an eight- or nine-hour day. The ladder work, of course, is easier than the field crops and as a result we do not get as tired.

Our last stop here [northeast Indiana] is picking tomatoes. We are not yet sure how much we will make. Tomatoes are very hard and slow because of the difference in ripening on the same plants.

What about your housing and food?

Well, that seems to trouble a lot of people; they seem to think every place should be an elegant motel. They don't quite have the feeling we have that if you are on the road you have to learn to accept what you run up against. Of course, a crew leader can complain and refuse to let his people stay in some of the dumps. But he is pretty helpless, especially since the main idea of their being there is to work and to make as much money as he can bargain for (the more he gets for them, the more he gets for himself). The ones who complain probably live in dumps just as bad at home. Now I tell you honestly [this is Pancho speaking], most of these people would not know how to keep up a real nice place, and certainly they are not going to learn while away from home in somebody else's place. Some of the wives and mothers try to fix up the quarters to make them a little better to live in. But, really, I think they expect too much.

An all-man crew is pretty well satisfied with what they find. Most of them just don't give a damn, and some of them are winos. They get along the best they can and you don't hear many complaints. Those of us traveling alone just take what we find.

You see, if a farmer doesn't want to sink a lot of money into nice houses or dormitories, only the state people can make them. There are supposed to be some United States regulations, but who is to make them obey? For one thing, you can understand why farmers don't want to put a lot of money into buildings which will only be used for a short time—sometimes the harvesters are only there for a few weeks in the whole year. Why should he bother to make them too comfortable?

One place where it was pretty lousy—dirty toilets, no washrooms, garbage everywhere (which the workers threw out without caring how it looked) and broken windows—the workers wanted to strike and they threatened to do it. You know what the farmer said? "Well, o.k. by me, go somewhere else to work. I can always get lousy foreigners like you to work without putting up with your complaints. So, if you don't like it, you know what you can do." A good many farmers just think of the Mexicans as work horses, and what should they care about giving them any comforts?

Now, *we* both take life as it comes. [Hector] My motto is get along no matter what. *I* didn't have to come, and I can leave any time I want to. As for the state laws, who knows what they are? I chose to get away from Texas each year, so I have to take everything that happens. Life is easier that way.

You should know that the dormitories with only men are sometimes pretty bad. These guys pay no attention to the rules that are posted. Lots never bathe, throw the food around, make garbage, play cards all night, gamble, have fist fights and don't pay any attention to other people and their comfort. The winos are the worst; if they have a pint of cheap muscatel they are happy. But as long as they do their work the crew leader and the farmer do not try to control them. The rest of us just put up with everything. But I do say that you want to work better for the farmers who have taken the trouble to give you good quarters to stay in.

Food? Most families buy their own stuff, and if mama cooks good they probably eat as well as they do at home. We two generally pool with some others and so we eat good. TV dinners, canned goods and so on, nothing fancy. There is always someone who wants to cook. Of course, if we want something special we can always hitch a ride to town, and we do this often, especially on weekends. However, there are not many Spanish restaurants around, so we do miss our kind of food.

What do we do for fun? Well, we read some, and we loaf and have a portable radio. Sometimes someone has a TV set. At two places where we were this year the farmers put TV sets in the dorm, and almost everyone watched it until bedtime; there was a bell which meant we had to be quiet. As far as fun in town is concerned, we are really too tired at night to bother much. A movie on weekends, or sometimes just walking around the town and drinking a few beers. One time a barman would not serve Hector here because he was not old enough—can you beat that? No, we never get drunk—well, hardly ever, and then only on weekends. We get guys at bars to buy us drinks and we make up stories about our experiences on our trips, so they buy drinks in order to listen some more.

But to most of the local people we are definitely outsiders. They look funny at us and call us spics; this is because most of us speak Spanish and, of course, we are darker. They seem to think we are some kind of foreigners who will be leaving soon. Oh, yes [Pancho], I was invited a few times to dinners in homes, but the people were not at ease with me. They tried hard, I know, but they seemed to think I led a funny kind of life and if I was a solid citizen I would stay on a regular job instead of doing dirty field work. I thought they looked at me as if I was going to steal their silverware (lots of people don't trust Mexicans or Puerto Ricans or Negroes). But at least they showed they meant well, and the food was good.

In a couple of towns some people invited us all—families and singles—to dances, so we got all dressed up and, though we didn't expect to, we had a good time. Some of the workers had guitars and some were singers and they put on a program. In one place they even had a Mexican combo which came from God knows where, and some of us taught those local girls how to dance Spanish-style! You never heard such stomping and shouting, and saw such wiggling in your life! In some towns there were classes for children, and they even picked up the boys and girls in station wagons and brought them back to the camps. So there are some good things, after all.

I suppose you will come back north next year?

Bet your life. You see, mister, this is our annual change. Life in Texas is not very exciting, and so we just live until we can start out again.

How did we make out this year? Well [Pancho], I am taking back about nine hundred dollars. I [Hector] have almost as much. Considering the time, that is not bad; at least it's better for the same time at home. Maybe one day we will quit, or perhaps we will settle down in the north, but certainly not in the country. It will be in a big city. Not right away, but some day.

From their stories, Pancho Rivera and Hector Gonzalez would seem to have found a way of life which for the present is both satisfactory and satisfying to them. They consider themselves completely independent, since they are "on their own." What their lives in Texas are like they chose not to reveal. It may be supposed that the annual trip is a way of breaking away from monotony (or perhaps, poverty).

A Family Plagued by Bad Luck *(La Suerte Mala)*

The family of Alberto Lopez were gathered around their battered 1956 model Dodge in a small work camp near

Laredo, Texas, when they agreed to talk about their experiences traveling as a unit in the northwest branch of the Central Stream. They had returned from the 1967 trip, from May to mid-October, in which they had journeyed almost two thousand miles, working locally in southwestern Texas and moving north to work in southeastern Colorado. Now they were again intrastate laborers, seeking work wherever it could be found in the lower Rio Grande Valley.

The trip could only be characterized as *un desastre* (a flop, a disaster); nothing seemed to have worked out. Work in Colorado was not as available as on previous trips—the Lopezes are eight-year veterans—because of *el tiempo malo* (the bad weather). This occurred not in Colorado but in California, where spring weather had delayed the harvests of several extensive crops which usually employed thousands of workers. According to the United States Department of Labor, areas were actually on the verge of disaster; six weeks of cold, wet weather in March and April had caused extensive damage to major crops and set back the time schedule on all farming activities. A hot spell in May, followed by rains in early June, caused floods, with the melting snow draining down from the mountains into the valleys. As a result, California migrant workers, both intra- and interstate, sought work wherever it could be found in other states outside the Pacific Coast Stream. Many hundreds made the long journey eastward over the Sierra Nevada Mountains through Nevada and Utah to Colorado. Texicans abandoned their plans to work in California, and made their way northward instead.

The Lopez family discovered that crews had taken over most of the available harvest jobs. Mr. Lopez had not made any advance plans. He seemed to be suspicious of the "government" men who might have helped him. Perhaps it was pride that made him continue to assert his usual independence, but instead of seeking assistance, he wandered aimlessly and with increasing desperation, following rumors which might lead him to a place where he and his family might find work.

He made the long return trip in complete desolation, ending up with only about one hundred sixty dollars to show for the family's five months of work. In December he was still searching for the reason why *El Dios* (God) had deserted him. He had come to the conclusion that he had been punished for some misdeeds or *pecados* (sins), yet try as he would he could not identify them. The obvious result was a burden of hopelessness and depression which he was unable to throw off.

The five-member family consisted of Alberto (in his midthirties), his wife Rosa (about thirty-two), and the children, Manuel (fourteen), Anita (twelve), and the three-year-old baby, Jesús. The two oldest children worked whenever they were allowed to; in several cases, Mr. Lopez had begged a farmer to give work to Manuel and Anita because money was so badly needed. The little money they thus earned had more than once provided them with food and gasoline.

The Lopez family was, it would seem, not at all typical. Yet their trials and distress appear to recur all too often in all the streams, particularly with those who are either unable or unwilling to plan, and therefore rely almost entirely on *la suerte* (luck) and *la esperanza* (hope). Their experiences form a pathetic tale of the hopelessness of poverty, the frequent frustrations of migrant farm workers, and the human misery resulting from the inability to find work.

With the exception of Rosa (Mrs. Lopez), the family all spoke recognizable English. Because of his schooling, even though it was irregular, Manuel's English was good, and he aided his father in the interview.

Tell me something about yourself and your family.

We are American citizen, all born in Texas. We live in Brownsville. This is long way south where Rio Grande is wide near ocean (Gulf of Mexico). Always I have work the crop many year, but never for myself. What crop? Everything from chop cotton to pick melon and cantaloupes; they very heavy. My back strong because of hard work. See the shoulder and muscle! I am *muy* strong. [He flexes his biceps to indicate his strength; his general appearance is one of vitality and health.] Back only now begin hurt from always lean over.

About eight, nine year ago some *amigos* say I earn moneys if I leave home on long trip far away to north. I have the auto and go to fields sometimes for one day, sometimes week or more; always I come back home. Rosa say she like try. Manuel have six year then, Anita little girl [four]. Jesús not yet here.

We start out, work many place but never make *mucho* moneys. But it be better than home and we be together. Sleep in auto alway, take blankets, dishes, and clothes in back [the car trunk], also some food like the bean, rice, and such. Some year good, some bad; we use *mucho* gas find work. Sign be on road and we look for, then stop. Rosa work *mucho,* with Anita sleep in auto. Manuel go to auto see if she o.k. We like change, go 'way from home, see differ[ent] place, meet peoples, always work. But this year be bad like never before. You want hear about? *Sí?*

Yes, tell me about this last trip.

Winter and spring I work the pepper, tomato, and cabbage along river [lower Rio Grande Valley]. Rosa sometime work too. I save the moneys start out in May. We drives north and finds only the onions dry [near the New Mexico state line]. We thin and pull, both. Anyways we works—all, even Anita, and it give enough monies to go on, which is in Colorado [southeast] again with the onions. We all has onion stink; it not wash off hand and even get in auto, make bad sleep. [They sleep in the car, Manuel says, to save money, even if there are accommodations available, for they have learned the necessity of always having *el dinero* [cash] to get to the next place, which might be a long trip. Also they are never sure of their next job.] We do this onion for long time [until August], then finds work in melon. Too hard for Rosa and Anita; the farmer not let them work.

This begin real trouble. We not know somewhere other because we not know where be work. We decide we stay, and the mens works. [Manuel stands straighter, almost bursting with pride that he is recognized as a man.] Not much moneys; in true very bad, only about fifty dollar week for both.

All these place not good for work. We think maybe we travel find better pay, but what do? All four needs work pay gas, car, food, and have money take home. Lots money for food, but Rosa say we need *la fuerza* [strength] for working. I *no comprendo* [understand] why we have *la suerte mala* [bad luck]. We lose *la esperanza* [hope]. We come home in October and I works again in the cabbage for the sauerkraut.

Do you plan where you will go?

Yes, we find out. How we know it depend on what peoples tell us. Reason we not go with other peoples is that family like be alone. Sometime people not right and we finds no work.

Will you go again next year?

Sí, siempre [always]. We think it not be so bad as this, so we try again. Maybe we goes next year in bus or truck in family or maybe I goes with Manuel. Or I goes with other mens. *But I goes.*

The urge to be on the move, which is one of the characteristics of the seasonal migrant, is irresistible in Alberto Lopez. So is his belief that the next trip will be more successful than the last. He calls it *la esperanza*. And, undaunted by his experiences, he will fight to keep this hope alive within him.

4

On the Season:
The Pacific Coast Stream

Disappointments, frustrations, and unhappiness are the unfortunate lot of the majority of migrants, particularly of those families who travel on their own. The contentment of crew members depends mainly upon their leader.

The story of the Santana family shows in contrast that the way of life of the interstate migrant on the season can be both happy and rewarding. This satisfaction, it should be pointed out, would appear to depend in part on the individuals involved—their general stability, the possession of sufficient funds both to aid them in the early stages of the trip and for use in emergencies, careful planning of a fixed schedule either through a responsible labor contractor (crew leader) or established federal and state farm labor employment offices (Chapter 6), and the ability to avoid discouragement when conditions fall short of their expectations. The resulting security makes them better and more contented workers.

A Happy Family

Miguel Santana and his family have found happiness in their seasonal journeys; the 1967 trip was their seventh. Their skins are dark, and the first impression one receives is of vigorous health and scrupulous cleanliness. These are the hallmarks of successful migrants, for discouragement and despondency lead to carelessness in the washing of both their bodies and their clothes.

The family consists of Miguel, who admits to forty years, his wife Elena (about thirty-five) and four children—Pedro, sixteen; Guillermo, fourteen; Felipe, eleven; and Maria, five. Miguel and Elena say their greatest happiness is their children, and they would never go anywhere without them. This is indeed a family of togetherness, where the parents, perhaps because of the common basis of their lives, are close to their offspring.

The Santanas are third-generation Mexican-Americans. Unlike most of their fellow Texicans, English is their preferred language, though they lapse into Spanish terms when they cannot find the English words to express what they mean. Among their own people they revert to their native tongue.

When interviewed in December, after the 1967 trip, they had returned to their home base, Laredo, on the Rio Grande River, the border of Mexico. The tape recorder was a focal point of interest to the entire family, and it was used in their parlor after a dinner of *tomamos* (soup), *paella* (rice with chicken), and a dessert. Elena beamed her satisfaction with the success of the dinner; as a matter of fact, she smiled constantly.

They were in high spirits because they were able to take a month's vacation for *la pascua* (the Christmas season). All the family made a contribution except little Maria.

Though commencing their trip from Texas, the major source of migrant seasonal workers in the Central Stream, the Santanas are among the growing number of Mexican-Americans following the Pacific Coast Stream and replacing the imported Mexican *braceros,* now practically nonexistent.

What about you and your family [to Mr. Santana]?

We is year-round harvest workers, except two boy who go school from time we get back from trip until we starts again. They works hard, and we thinks they deserve rest and have the education; perhaps they find other work when they grown. Pedro is like *un mecanico* and he do all repair on automobile [a 1958 model which they do not use for their local work], and he want learn work in garage. We live in thees small wood house here; you see it not be much but Elena keep clean, always wash floors and other works. We have two bedroom. The boys have two bed, Maria sleep with us. Furniture good, but not fancy, *sí?*

When not away I, Elena sometime, works in fields near. [This is day-haul, but sometimes long-haul when Miguel travels longer distances, often twenty-five miles each way.] I never be gone overnight on thees works. Last winter I works in beans, carrots, and spinach. Knows many friends. Truck pick up in plaza and bring back. Pay good, differed for differed things. [The "good" pay averages about $1.30 per hour.]

The troubles [strikes occurred at the same time in Texas as in California] last year not be here; it far south near river and in melon, which I never works at home. Thees work hard, but all work in fields be hard. No, I not like, but what do? I have not education do something else, so what I does I does good. Ask anyone, and they say, "That Miguel, he good, glad have him."

How did you happen to start traveling?

About long year ago I talk to mans work with me. He go on trips, and he say, "Why you work always here near home? I know good mans who take peoples and famblies in big bus and we is treat well. We travels and brings back the monies—*muy bueno* [very good]. Want see him?" So I talks with mans and he tell about plan for spring—six place end in California. Elena and I we decide try. Pedro have eight year, Guillermo six, and Felipe very little [three]. It work nice for change. We have much happiness and so go ever year. *El patron* always same. [His name was never mentioned, not even as Señor X, perhaps indicating the respect the Santanas have for him as their employer.]

Tell me about this trip.

Use be excite when start. Now regular, know what take. Same bus (new for four year), same peoples, lots childrens, same *patron*. We is almost fifty. *El patron* have big auto and house [trailer], his son have auto too, and carry *el equipaje* [baggage] in back [trailer]. Bus have plenty room. We use to childrens cry, no bother us. Stop often, rest, and use *excusado* [toilet].

"Elena, where we go?" [*His wife brings out the book with their schedule.*]

The crew traveled westward from Texas through New Mexico, where they harvested lettuce during May, then on to central Arizona for six weeks picking cantaloupes, then into California. After spending the last two weeks of July in the southeast part of the state near the Mexican border, they continued in the melon fields, then moved to the southern end of the San Joaquin Valley, northeast of Los Angeles, picking tomatoes during the long season from August until October fifteenth.

El patron choose what we do, and we no surprise. Example: we has melon, it hard for Elena. [Some farmers will not permit women to work in the melon fields.] So what we do? Elena not work all time, depend how she feel. Guillermo work little, too hard, he just *muchacho* [*He rumples his son's hair*]. So both rest and be ready for *el tomate.* Health be better. Pedro and me works harder in these time.

La vida en esta temporado [Life during this season]? *El patron* fix all. We not have the worry. When get to work place, bus stop, he go see farmer. They all *sonrisa* [smiles], he *muy feliz* [very happy] see us. We not stranger, this be fourth time we comes. They talk, *el patron* go with bus, see houses. We wait settle. If not o.k., he go back, see farmer and it be fix.

But most time farmer have good place, take care. *El patron* park auto and house near us so he be help. He tell when we leave and we ready. He collect monies by week and give ever[y]one. We not take all, he save for us at end; this way we not spend. He say we is his childrens, and childrens spends all monies foolish and he want us have monies for home.

What we picks? Sometime change by year [year by year] when machines come. But machines cost *mucho,* and farmers like us work [an indication of the imperative necessity for human labor, even when mechanization (Chapter 11) is partially used in harvesting].

Now, for *la lechuga* [lettuce]. Heads is ready at differd times, in rows some little, some big. They is tender, and machines is rough. So we picks and we moves boxes with us [along the rows], and they takes away when full. We gets thirty cents box, not pay by hour [the hourly rate is from $1.25 to $1.50].

Hard work begin with melon. They be differd ripe and big and little, heavy and light. We learn feel see if almost ripe, must pick when green and hard so week-ten day they be right in *el mercado* [market]. Shoulder get tire[d] because of heavy. Elena work only 'bout half. [The crew picked melons for eight weeks.] Pay by hour about best, $1.35; this because heavy work.

Next we go three hundred mile for *el tomate* and stay ten week. Long time, not work at same farm but differds. Stay about six place, go back to three. Every one except Maria work *el tomate.* They not too bad but hard on knee[s]. We have *la protección* [large wraparound knee pads] we wears. Sometime ground wet and get much dirty.

El tomate take much time since we selects for ripe and size.

The sort they do late[r]. Two field we pick three time in all. This
for stores. [Two-thirds of the total California crops is to be
canned and is mechanically harvested.] We most gets the hour
rate near two dollar. Two time we get thirty cent for fifty
pound, that lot of *tomate* for pay, but when we works together
it be 'bout same as for hour. We likes *el tomate* best 'cause we
talks while work; if work alone it be not good.

Work over. Bus ride back, long time, no work, rest night.
Monies? Yes, after pay *el patron* [what they owe] we have
twelve hundred dollar. This good and make winter easy. Childrens late school, Guillermo and Felipe go 'til begin next spring
trip. Pedro not go, maybe when old[er] he go learn autos
[mechanics].

What about your life on the trips [to Mrs. Santana]?

With good man [*she beams at Miguel*] and good *patron* we
have a good life. No problem.

Food? I good cook, not cost too much. We has all the good
things. [She reels off in Spanish some of her specialties.] Never
hungry, important for work.

Where we stay? We with friend fambly near, make like one
fambly. Señora Del Rio have two baby, she watch Maria all
time I gone. I no have to pay. She take to health place in some
town[s]. White *señores* very nice. Maria play, go in bus with
other childrens. [*El patron* uses his bus on weekdays for this,
after he takes the workers to the fields, then returns the children
just before he picks up his crew to take them "home."]

All houses good, mostly. Once we comes to thees one place—
I not tell you where or when—and right then I sees it be a bad
place. I know in five minute, maybe, always if it be good. This
be *awful*. There be paper [tar paper] all torn on outside, window
be broke and pile trash, *latas* (cans), lots paper everywhere. No
clean after other before leave. We get *el patron* and he have
fix; then all o.k. We have the gas and the hot water. I carry
blanket[s] and mattress in *el patron* auto.

Most house clean, some with lots famblies, some in long row
with own door. Some with trees and grass and some special toilet
and bath houses. Some better than our own *casa*. This one reason we like go California.

Schools? They is places for childrens to learn, but we send only when melon pick. They not learn much because they strangers. But we not worry since they be took care of. Remember, they go school all time at home.

Will you go next year?

Sí, sí, sí. We already sign in words with *el patron. La vida de la temporada* o.k. *Estos ultimos años* [these last few years] be very happy. We not be afraid work, and while we be strong we go.

The reasons for the Santanas' satisfaction is obvious. The key to their success is due largely to the work of their *patron,* who in this case would seem to be somewhat of a model. [He could not be interviewed, since he was not in Texas at the time.] His labor-contract planning permitted him to tell them in advance where and when they would work, and their wages and financial arrangements were made known to them. In other words, they were secure. And security is what most seasonal farm workers lack.

A Teen-age Fruit Picker and His Family

During the 1967 harvest season, Juan Mendez and his family, traveling by truck, covered about twenty-five hundred miles. This mileage is unusual even for the vast distances in the Pacific Coast Stream. (A crew leader in the Central Stream fixed the average at about fifteen hundred to 1,750 miles, and in the Pacific Coast Stream at about twelve to fifteen hundred miles when a trip is made from Texas to southern California.) Since riding in the bed of a truck is, to say the least, uncomfortable, one can realize the added physical strain of the orchard work. As Juan put it, "The long, bumpy trips make so we arrive already tired, yet we must right away begin the hard work. If we had to pick on the ground, I doubt if we could keep up from day to day. But on the ladder it is some easier."

The migrant life has been the family's lot for four years. Juan is the eldest son (seventeen) and the man of the family since his father died four years ago. The brood which he guides on the annual trek includes his mother Serafina (whom he calls mama) and two younger brothers, Alberto (fifteen) and Rafael (thirteen and a half). Since picking fruit is their sole occupation, Juan has apparently never considered any alternative to following the crops.

The two younger boys have attended school only long enough to learn the most basic English, and Spanish is spoken within the family since Mrs. Mendez speaks no other language. Surprisingly, Juan's English is quite good; he explains this by the fact that he wants to learn as much English as possible so that when he "settles down" he will not be considered a "foreigner." He therefore acted as spokesman for the group when interviewed at their small tar-papered house near Linden, California, not far from Stockton, at the northern end of the San Joaquin Valley. The area produces a variety of crops, and when "home," Juan works on both day- and long-haul picking assignments.

Attempts to pinpoint the exact localities where the Mendez family worked proved fruitless. Unlike the families who travel under a crew leader who feel it necessary to maintain a record of places worked and their earnings, or those who travel as singles in automobiles and must therefore consult maps to reach localities where work is available, Juan admitted that he had no idea whatever of town names. He knew only in what areas of the states covered—California, Oregon, and Washington—he and his family had worked, and sometimes not even that. A United States Farm Labor Service crop map containing a key to the harvest periods of various fruits served to aid him somewhat in reconstructing the approximate areas where they had worked. He obviously possessed little ability in map reading; he knew only the direction in which he traveled. "The driver," he said, "gets us there and we ask no questions. All places the same: trees, fruit, ladders, shoulder and back aches, but money, yes, I remember that!" One wonders how many of the thousands of interstate workers have any idea of where they are at a given time; as with the Mendezes, this may be unimportant to them.

Indeed, the details of the periods spent picking the different fruits are blurred. Almost like a robot, Juan and his family move from orchard to orchard, do their work, which varies only in the type of "spot" picking, climb up and down the ladders, rest, and move on. The routines become monotonous, and, almost like ghostly figures, they walk through the mechanics of their lives.

From the descriptions of the crops they picked, the Mendez family apparently worked north through the Sacramento Valley, passing into southwest Oregon near Medford, then north between Eugene and Salem, then into Washington state, past Vancouver, and eastward along the southern boundary to the farthest point of their trip in southeast Washington. As ladder workers, they picked a great variety of fruits, including peaches, pears, plums, cherries, apples, and apricots. They are indeed specialists.

How did you start taking your yearly trips?

When my father died [*crosses himself*] I became the head of the family, even though I was only thirteen years old. In Mexican families, the oldest son always take the dead father's place. I was big for my age—you would think I was at least twenty right now, wouldn't you? [and indeed anyone would, for he is tall and slim, and gives an impression of maturity far beyond his chronological age] and no one asked any questions, so I became *un hombre!* Mama was not very strong, so I did not want her to work hard for us (while my father was sick she took in washing). Since I had picked fruit with my father during the school vacations, I got a daytime job in an orchard near town. They needed help and no one asked my age, so it was easy. The school man [truant officer] came around to see mama and ask where I was, but she said I was working far away (he came in the daytime), and finally he stopped coming. Alberto and Rafael told them the same thing when he asked them.

I was picking cherries (it was in May) and one day a man stopped me and said, "You are a good worker, yes? You like your work? Want to go on trip with me to earn much more money than you make here?" And he told me of the picking to the north a long ways. I said I had a family to take care of. He told about his truck and said they could go along if they wanted to pick fruit. We would be two or three other families and would all work together. He made no promises and I didn't ask him.

So in the middle of July we all got into the truck. We sat on the side benches or lay on the mattresses on the floor, and the whole front part was filled with baggage, bedding, and stuff. There were twenty of us crowded together. Well, that year we went far north and stayed in about seven places in all kinds of cabins and shacks, but we came back in November with money. I think it was about five hundred dollars, more than we had ever had before. Even the boys had earned some, though they could not pick or work as fast as mama and me.

The boys went back to school, but always we left with the summer vacation and returned after the school had begun again. Mama finally talked to the people and said we all had to work, but she would try to have them go when they were home in Linden. Some people stayed in our house while we were away; they always do.

Tell me about this trip.

We go with the same man, Mr. Fernandez, in the same truck. After the first trip we got used to it. We follow him because he is a man you follow. At bottom he is for his people. He does not tell us much, sits in front with the driver. The farmers who hire him understand that all the children must work. He does not take babies, and the youngest this year was nine, but sometimes he did not work.

The children do not pick but hold the ladders and give us new baskets or pails and take the full ones to the [pickup] trucks where they are taken to the sheds for sorting. Each one take care of about two trees, about six people, so they are busy running back and forth. They are not paid very much but it helps.

We were about twenty this trip. Five families with ten mens and womens, the rest childrens. No one gets sick at all, but they all gets tired. Sometimes there is a long ride between jobs and we travel at night because it is cool. Everyone sleeps and most can go to sleep sitting just as if they were in bed. The driver is the son of Mr. Fernandez, and he has the radio on so he will not fall asleep; many wrecks when trucks go off the road. Sometimes we get to the farm at early morning and start work while the womens unpack and arrange the houses.

We leave Linden in early June and go first just a little way to pick peaches. We pick only the big yellow (with red) ripe ones ["spot" picking] because all are not ready at the same time. These were early, and later there would be more for others to pick. We did not have to be careful because they were for canning. Some of the women worked in the factory [cannery] nearby, peeling them. Money? I don't know, Mr. Fernandez collect and give.

After three weeks, I think, we go north in short trip and pick plums for a month [June 15–July 15?]. These are for stores, so we have to watch. Then close by we pick pears for a month [July 15–August 15?]. Then I think we go to Oregon for more pears (it is the same season).

From here on, Oregon and Washington appear to be interchangeable to Juan, and the "I thinks" become more frequent. However, he recalls that they picked cherries in Oregon (he does not remember the time), apricots in either

Oregon or Washington, and, definitely, pears (again) and, finally, apples as late as November first.

We came home without stopping to work. It was a long ride, about four days, I think, and we had to pay extra to sleep in places where the cabins were not being used. Mr. Fernandez just turned into farms in the late afternoon, and asked if we could stay. Since he wanted to make time, we drove during the daytime.

How much we bring back this time? I know not right, but I ask mama here. . . . About seven hundred dollars for the four. Of course, we paid for food, but Mr. Fernandez paid for the houses. I think he makes much money, but when we say we should get more he say, "Not possible." He cry that he be poor. This not true, I am sure, because he have nice home and big car and run truck all year. But what to do?

What about your life on the road?

[The question seems to puzzle him. When housing, food, and health are suggested, he confers with his mother, but she proves noncommittal. Evidently to them nothing appeared to be exceptional.]

The houses? Some good, some bad. But really, mister, we not want talk about that. No, I am not afraid but do not want your print [book] have any complaint. Mr. Fernandez not like. California not bad; we even had some nice cement houses. With three men and mama it be necessary when we stay as one family that she sleep with Rafael, because most places has two big [double] beds. Oregon and Washington good and bad; some were tin and it was still hot all night. Some cabins [one-family units] were not very clean. How much? Mr. Fernandez pay and take from what he give us. Some peoples carry tents, and maybe we do next year.

Food? Mama cooks and we eat like at home. Nothing special.

Health? We have no trouble, for we are healthy family. Some people who get sick are sent to the towns and they get care, medicines and such.

Towns? We have no time to go and Mr. Fernandez not like to take us. He say we are on trip to work, not play. Sometimes we stop to buy food and walk around and rest legs.

Oh, yes, he has a radio which we get to play outside the bus. But we have to listen together, so if we want to hear, we listen in front of one of the houses. Sometimes we divided and one family has for a few days, another for a few days. Maybe I buy one for us alone next year.

Will you go again?

Yes, of course. Each year get better and we used to it. We will pick again what Mr. Fernandez has for work. I often think maybe we stay in California instead of go, but the change is good. But California always good to go back to.

For the Mendez family, life on the season has obviously become a routine. They pay little attention to where they go and what they do. Mr. Fernandez is a practical, somewhat unapproachable crew leader who has trained them to accept conditions without question. The dreariness and monotony of their lives is unvaried. The pattern is the same: work and more work.

5

Getting the Work

Every large-scale grower, whether an individual or a corporate farmer with extensive acreage, depends upon specially recruited temporary workers when the vast crops are ready to harvest. At such times the regular working force, whether a few permanent hired hands on a single large farm or the many hundreds of agribusiness employees who plant and tend the crops until they reach the peak of their development, must be supplemented by seasonal help with harvest laborers to pick the crops.

During the height of the 1967 summer harvests (June through August) in the United States, the number of temporary workers was a little over a million. The largest number of these workers were students who worked during the vacation period until the reopening of school. They numbered about half a million in 1967.

A grower can recruit four types of workers for the peak harvest periods: (1) local, (2) intrastate, (3) interstate, and (4) foreign.

The first type—local workers—is made up of both students and local residents, including many women. They are known as "day-haul" workers or commuters to the fields. In this program, previously selected workers are assembled at designated pickup points and transported to and from their jobs in trucks or buses. They represented 79 percent of the total workers throughout the country in the summer of 1967. Such workers form the largest number of seasonal laborers; in California, for example, in 1966, 90,000 out of 120,000, about three-quarters in the state, were local workers.

The second type is called intrastate, defined as migratory workers who make short journeys within a state, often within the same county or adjoining areas, who may stay at a place of work for a few days or a longer period, or may travel from farm to farm but never across state boundaries. They are never as far away from their homes as those migrants who make the long seasonal trips; in other words, they do not follow the crops for great distances. California, with its vast distances, places great reliance on workers who migrate within its boundaries; in 1966 a monthly average of 20,000 were being hired, and at the peak period in September 35,000 were at work. The peak for Texas, another vast state, was 23,000 in July.

The total number of interstate migrant workers, the third type and the subject of this book, can only be approximated because of the large number of family and single workers not tallied in official statistics. In 1967, the highest number reported at work at one time was nearly a quarter of a million, but the number was actually much higher, and a total of 350,000 is generally considered a more realistic figure. This incomplete figure for interstate workers emphasizes the nomadic nature of their lives and work, and has led them to be called "America's undetermined minority." Yet these are the wanderers who feed us all.

Twenty percent of all summer workers in 1967 were migrants, both intra- and interstate.

The importation of foreign workers, the fourth type, is increasing and beginning to offer genuine competition to the interstate migrants. The total number in 1967 was 31,000, 9,000 of whom were employed in Florida, 6,100 in California *(braceros),* and 3,200 in Maine. Ten thousand were employed in the Middle Atlantic states.

Foreign workers are contracted for by growers whose harvest schedules are so crucial that they do not wish to rely upon the workers from the South. Many feel that the risks involved in not knowing for sure whether the interstate migrants will arrive at the exact time and be dependable can be eliminated by securing highly selected groups under crew leaders of guaranteed effectiveness, made possible by the payment of higher wages and the meeting of conditions of work definitely stated in contracts. Since the expense to the grower is greater, he can reasonably anticipate a superior work force.

Puerto Ricans are being increasingly imported under contracts made with the Puerto Rico Labor Department through the New York and Florida regional offices of the United States Farm Labor Service. Rigid conditions of employment are agreed upon. Such men—families are not permitted to accompany them—are flown in by plane. Puerto Ricans worked in Michigan during 1967, and New Jersey used them extensively, particularly in the harvesting of asparagus and tomatoes.

Florida usually employs West Indians and Bahamians in addition to Puerto Ricans. In Maine, Canadians are imported for the short period of the potato harvest, since none of the interstate migrants in the Atlantic Stream travel that far north.

The uncertainty of the weather is a constant enemy of growers, crew leaders, and the workers themselves. The best-laid plans made far in advance can be and are often thwarted by unpredictable developments which upset the harvest schedules. As a result, hundreds of interstate migrants become idle until the date of their next work contracts where the crop cycle has not been interrupted. However, some crew leaders are able quickly to locate work in other sections of a state or a region and move their workers to them. At such periods, the individual or family workers traveling alone find themselves stranded far from home, often without funds and with little hope for the future. They can only move on in the hope that they will have good luck in their search for work.

Throughout the United States, vagaries in the weather in 1967 were almost unprecedented. In some sections the results proved disastrous to farmers and, therefore, to migrant workers.

California was particularly hard hit during 1967. The unseasonable spring weather, which damaged many crops, had repercussions throughout the year. The state's output of fruit decreased considerably. (Incidentally, the housewife-consumer was immediately affected by a sizable price increase in canned and uncanned fruits and some vegetables.) The grape crop was down 21 percent from 1966, the pear crop was only one-third as large as that of the preceding year, peach production dropped by a fifth, and one-third fewer apples were harvested.

In September, Hurricane Beulah damaged citrus and vegetable crops in the lower Rio Grande Valley of Texas. In New Jersey, the excess rains slowed the late summer harvesting, and crops such as onions, tomatoes, green beans, and blueberries lagged for two weeks behind the anticipated dates.

Such conditions inevitably result in a substantial reduction in seasonal work opportunities. All workers suffer, but the effect on those far from home is particularly severe, upsetting plans, dashing hopes for an overall financially successful season, and producing both discouragement and desperation.

While weather is the migrant's temporary enemy, a far greater threat is the increasing mechanization of agriculture, discussed in Chapter 11.

The "forgotten people" of the interstate migrant population are the estimated 10 percent who do not travel as members of a crew. Hundreds of loners or freewheelers travel as singles, like the teen-agers Pancho Rivera and Hector Gonzalez in the Central Stream (Chapter 3). Other loners like the Smiths in the Atlantic Stream (Chapter 2) and the Lopez family in the Central Stream (Chapter 3) travel by automobile with their families who may or may not work. Such migrants generally suffer greatly from a lack of organization which almost always leads to disappointing earnings, aimless wandering, substandard housing, and, finally, disillusionment and frustration. They seldom take advantage of the excellent state and federal government services available under the Annual Worker Plan of the United States Department of Labor. Their insecurity is obvious, their desperation understandable, and their financial returns negligible. (One study gives $190 as the average earnings of a family of four for a season of four months.) These laborers are all too often the victims of unscrupulous growers, for they must accept conditions of work and rates of pay which are both intolerable and unjust. Like those who work for unprincipled crew leaders who manage to avoid the federal regulations, they are exploited unmercifully.

Ninety percent of the interstate migrant workers, even those accompanied by all or part of their families, as well as most intrastate, local, and foreign workers, travel and work as crew members. The crew leader, alternately called the labor contractor, is therefore the key to both the workers' achievement and their mode of life. He holds the power of the success or failure of his charges in their earnings, and his effectiveness influences their morale and well-being.

6

Key Man:
The Crew Leader

The crew leader, as the middleman between the grower and the workers, is responsible for recruiting and hiring, transportation to the various work areas and even daily to the fields, and the overall supervision of the work. He is a combination of policeman, father, banker, and boss. In the fields he oversees the workers but does no work himself. He often becomes a disciplinarian as well as a helpful adviser.

Sometimes called labor contractor, the crew leader is the key to both intrastate and interstate employment. Until very recently too many were racketeers skilled in bilking their charges. Following congressional hearings during 1963, a year in which much legislation regarding migrant workers was enacted, the Farm Labor Contractor Registration Act was passed, to take effect on January 1, 1965. Similar laws and regulations were already in force in eight states—California, Colorado, Nevada, New Jersey, New York, Oregon, Pennsylvania, and Washington—and this law was intended to cover all states uniformly.

In the text, crew leaders are defined as "those who make arrangements between workers and growers for interstate

96

agricultural employment." The law applies to "any person who recruits, solicits, hires, furnishes, or transports for a fee ten or more migratory workers for employment across state lines." The law requires their licensing by the United States Department of Labor and annual reports of activities, with penalties for non-compliance.

The duties of a contractor as outlined require that he keep payroll records and give employees wage and withholding statements, and specific information in regard to their employment at the time of recruitment—wages, schedule, type of work, expenses, etc.—and post a copy of the terms and conditions of work. When he is responsible for providing housing, he must post the terms and conditions of his agreement with each grower. These provisions were intended to correct the widespread exploitation of interstate migrant workers.

Too often, crews have traveled in buses discarded because of their condition and purchased at bargain prices by crew leaders, in dilapidated and broken-down trucks, both farm and commercial and of ancient vintage, and in all types of makeshift motor vehicles. They have undergone both acute discomfort and crowding. As many as forty men, women, and children have been regularly penned into the trucks for a trip of a thousand or more miles, often sitting or lying on the floors.

The obsolescence of motors and the inexperience and carelessness of the drivers have caused many serious, often fatal, accidents. In California, between 1952 and 1961, 112 farm workers were killed and 2,575 injured while being transported to and from jobs. Major accidents were frequent, due to defective brakes, collisions, and turnovers. One of the worst accidents occurred in 1957, when a truck carrying 41 migrant workers crashed in North Carolina. The death toll was 21. Later in that year the Interstate

Commerce Commission adopted a safety code for transportation of migrants. Among other requirements was one that a secure seat be furnished for each passenger. Enforcement, however, was lax.

Accidents continued to occur with alarming frequency. The worst was in 1963; 27 Mexican-Americans were killed and over 30 hurt when a makeshift bus was rammed by a freight train in Salinas, California.

In 1963, the Commission issued federal regulations for crew leaders, drivers, and owners of motor vehicles transporting workers. These included driver qualifications, standards for the comfort and safety of passengers, rules for meal and rest stops, and limitations in distances of uninterrupted travel.

These two landmark laws, if enforced, should eventually better the lives of the migrants in their charge. Within recent years, more and more leaders have chartered buses which comply with these regulations.

Recruiting by crew leaders is undertaken in many different ways. An experienced leader may learn of possible workers through the recommendation of those who have been with him previously. Or he may interview pickers working in local fields during the winter and those in his day-haul crews. He may visit stores, taverns, and other local spots to locate interested individuals or to obtain clues to possible workers. An efficient labor contractor realizes that it is to his benefit to brief his prospective employees in detail on such questions as places to be visited, pay scales, and housing and food problems so that no misunderstandings will occur. Even a good crew leader has an inevitable turnover in personnel, but he generally retains a core of experienced workers on whom he can rely.

The work of the United States Department of Labor is an absolute essential to both growers and labor contractors.

An advance activity of its Bureau of Employment Security is the prediction of harvests of various crops. The Farm Labor Service, a branch of the Bureau, annually issues a large wall map, *Peak Seasonal Farm Labor Force and Crop Production Centers.* By consulting this map and its accompanying manual a crew leader who plans a trip on the Atlantic Coast Stream, for example, is able to determine exact localities where workers are needed, and thus arrange his schedule through the various state and local offices of the Bureau.

A second major publication, useful to both crew leaders and individual workers, is a series of four *Guides to Seasonal Farm Work Areas*—Eastern Seaboard States (Atlantic Coast Stream), Gulf to the Great Lakes, Intermountain States (the two for the Central Stream), and Far Western States (Pacific Coast Stream). By examining the information given, the crew leader can contact the state and local employment offices to draw up contracts.

These services are basic to crew leaders, who are thus able to schedule work far in advance and to tell their recruits exactly where and how long they will work at a specific place, as well as the type of crop they will be harvesting.

Many crew leaders, like Mike Bishop under whom the Lee family worked (Chapter 2) and Amos, the leader of the crew which included Mrs. Jones, the beanpicker (also Chapter 2), are considerate of their charges and like fathers to them. However, all too often crew leaders are scoundrels and profiteers who exploit their charges.

Tales of abuses abound, and are far from secret; the federal law already described imposes punishment for such acts. But most crew workers are hesitant to oppose a leader or to reveal incidents of maltreatment or abuse. In-

stead, through fear of reprisal and a realization of the
futility of opposition, they accept his actions complacently
and unquestioningly. Some intimations of their resentment,
however, may be found mildly and somewhat timidly expressed in the case studies of migrants in at least two of the
streams. The interview in this chapter with the Mexican-
American crew leader, José Montero, constitutes a valid
picture of a conniving, ruthless, heartless, and authoritarian
crew leader in contrast to Mike Bishop, working on the
Atlantic Coast Stream.

Fortunately, studies of the migrant farm labor problem
invariably include descriptions of exploitation. The worker,
whatever his attitude toward his boss, usually sets out in
financial bondage to him. Most migrants possess little or
no money at the start of the trip and must borrow from the
man who recruits them. They are therefore under obligation to him from the beginning. The leader without conscience uses this situation to "keep them under control,"
particularly if the sum is not soon repaid. The better
leaders, like Mike Bishop, do not use such debts as a club
over their charges.

The intimidation may continue all along the way. Many
leaders receive a commission on their workers' output. This
practice, for example, has been exposed in New Jersey,
where for every fifteen cents that a worker earns by picking
a basket of tomatoes, the crew leader gets four or five cents.
This may prove to be a considerable source of his income,
and invariably has not been mentioned in his agreements
with crew members.

Scores of leaders are also loan sharks. When workers
need advances in their pay, they are charged enormous and
illegal interest rates, often up to 50 percent, and these
must be paid without dispute. Some leaders either operate
the food concession or receive a percentage from the grower

on purchases, and this results in higher prices charged. The profit on cheap wine is mentioned elsewhere.

Other unscrupulous leaders fail to bother themselves with the legal benefits legislated for farm workers. They pay no attention to social security payments and workmen's compensation—not only because of the amount of paper work involved, but also from a reluctance to inform their workers of their eligibility for such assistance.

A crew leader's earnings for the out-of-state harvest season may run well over ten or fifteen thousand dollars or as low as one thousand dollars, depending on the quality of the harvest and the size of his work force. By the season's end he may earn more than ten to fifteen times as much as one of his ablest workers.

The two interviews with crew leaders which follow may be considered as a study in contrasts.

An Eastern Stream Crew Leader

Mike Bishop, leader of the Atlantic Coast crew which included the Lee family (Chapter 2), is a personable Negro in his early fifties, who has organized crews and traveled with them on annual trips north for many years. The 1967 journey was his seventeenth and their fourteenth. At the time of the Lee interview in early September, the crew of 110 workers and their 65 dependents, both working and nonworking children and wives, had been on the road since the middle of May. Some of the older teen-agers worked more or less regularly, and are included in the total of workers.

Mike may properly be called an "old hand." Throughout the years he has perfected his leadership functions, and his annual plans follow a regular pattern and routine. The undertaking is thoroughly outlined in early March, and he is thus able to inform the workers with whom he makes contracts of what they may expect. Rarely, he says, does his plan go awry, and then only because of unpredictable weather, or when growers purchase mechanical harvesters for their particular crops in early spring, thus eliminating the need for a full crew of workers. In such cases, Mike never splits up his crew; he knows well the ins-and-outs of his business, and on the basis of his established reputation can always contract with another grower in approximately the same locality.

He and his wife travel with the crew from Florida, where he recruits the majority of his crew members, who have been working during the winter. As in the case of the Lees, however, he has also signed up other "regulars" from Georgia and Alabama. The turnover is about the average; approximately 25 percent make only a single trip and must be replaced each year. Most of these new workers come to him on the recommendation of his hard-core veterans or regulars.

The Bishops have invested in a small trailer which is attached to their late-model automobile. They live in the trailer parked near the fields; only rarely are his crew members housed near his camp site. He does this to maintain continuous contact with the grower. He is with his crew during their hours of work, and maintains that his relationship is better when he is "on call" from the camp. Crew leaders who live near the camp, he says, often create an impression of prying into the private lives of their charges, and he wishes to avoid this.

Before undertaking his first trip in 1950, he was a successful Georgia farmer. When his land, with adjoining acreage, was purchased by a large cotton company, the management established a full-time corps of local workers for planting, "chopping," and warehouse work at harvest time. He was offered year-round work with them, but he decided, as he explains, "to try my hand at being a boss rather than being bossed." He investigated the possibilities through the state office of the United States Farm Security Administration, now called the Farm Labor Service of the Department of Labor.

He evidently created a good impression—this was before the federal law (1965) requiring the registration of interstate farm labor contractors—and he obtained valuable advice on how to establish his new business. He purchased three fifty-passenger buses from a transportation company which had ceased operations, and had them reconditioned. From then on he learned through experience, and is now obviously a superior and successful professional crew leader.

Let him tell the story of his 1967 crew.

The United States laws which made my job easier were passed in 1963, and the 1965 trip was the first in which I had some definite rules to follow. (Even now lots of leaders fail to follow these regulations, "getting by" with only such control as the various states insist on.) Many states are very careless in checking on our work, and a leader can get away with murder if he wants to. This has given us a bad name which we have to overcome by performance.

During the winter season in Florida (from November to May), I run a "day haul" with my buses, which I have purchased and replaced from time to time. (There are now some strict government [federal] laws which we are supposed to obey.) Every morning before it is light, I dispatch my buses filled with day workers to the fields from a loading center, and bring them back at the end of each day. (I live in a central Florida town.) Generally I have the same workers—no families —who stick with me while the picking is good. We do no work in citrus fruits, for that is almost entirely done by machines in Florida. Instead it is celery, corn, beans, and all sorts of vegetables, called truck crops. We never work more than twenty-five miles away, as there is plenty of need that near.

By mid-February I have obtained the government estimated requirements for the summer and fall harvests in the northern states, and having been in the business so long, I make contact with my regular customers, the growers. They tell me how many workers they will want and when they are needed, and I sign a contract which states the dates, wages, and types of crops. I do this on a straight fee for the entire job, and it usually lets me estimate my profit from the job. I follow up on these contracts before we leave.

I do the recruiting near my home base. About half my workers are already working in my day-hauls. Leaving my drivers (and my wife and my grown son, who is my assistant) to take care of them, I travel around to sign up the others I need. I have regular customers like the Lees quite far away, and I would rather take the same people, whose work I know, if at all possible. Sometimes I pick up new people whom I hear of by word of mouth; that is, they have been recommended by my regulars who will vouch for them. (I have lots of cousins and in-laws in the crew.) The state offices [there are twenty-three throughout the state] also help me in certain localities in Florida.

By early April, or even before, I have my schedule completely organized and continue signing up my crew until it is full. Some are loners, because families add a lot of troubles. However, I have found that family men and their wives and older children are the most responsible workers. About 40 of the 110 crew members are single men.

I plan to fill my four buses, and the rest follow along in their own automobiles. Some of the families travel in the buses, but I limit them to four—the parents and at most two children. I warn those having their own cars to be sure the autos are in tip-top shape, because breakdowns are not only expensive to them, but also may force them to delay their arrival at the work place. The buses are not entirely filled because I use the big back seat and other seats near the rear for the baggage (these Negroes carry lots of stuff with them, particularly the families).

You might call me their father, because they depend more or less on me. All are colored, and they have to be treated like children. Helping them by advancing money, settling them down in the camps, seeing that they have what they need, and toting them to and from the fields and watching them at work is, let me tell you, certainly a full-time job!

I run one bus each evening after dinner to the nearest town (on weekends maybe two or three), and the drivers—I have had practically the same drivers for eight or nine years—wait to bring them back to the camps. I keep informed about all the government and local rules, and I find schools and day-care for the children and medical services when needed. I also get the townsfolk to give parties and entertainments so that my people will feel more at home. This all takes patience which, God be praised, I do have. Lots of leaders don't give a damn about anything but the work done, but I feel it all pays off, and, after all, my profit depends on my crew. I am paid on the spot by each grower, so few of my workers have money troubles. If they do, I give them an advance, knowing I can be repaid from the money they earn.

Their pay? Well, my crew do much better than average. I keep money for some of them who want to save and not have the temptation to spend all they earn along the way. Some send their money regularly back to their homes to be put in the bank. I don't know exactly how much they clear while on the trip, since it all depends on what they spend, but I think each worker makes from eight hundred to a thousand (and even more for some) dollars for the six months. This is about as much as they would make in Florida. Remember that they have current expenses. I clear several thousand dollars on the trip. (I won't tell you how much. I have put two children through college and helped two others in their family setups.)

I also help with the social security papers and payments. In fact, I do almost everything. My wife is very good with the women and their problems of family and children.

My aim is to help keep my crew happy. I think that, without boasting, I do a good job. There are always some unhappy workers and a few no-goods, but my conscience is clear. I will continue these trips and the Florida day-hauls until I am ready to retire, which will be some years from now. I probably have a little of a wandering feeling (I don't like to be tied down in one place all year), so I will be back as long as I am making a good profit and can take my job in stride.

A Leader Who Exploits His Crew

José Montero (not his real name) has been a crew leader working in the Central Stream for fifteen years. He admits frankly that "Business has been good; I might say it has been sensational." Why? "Well, after two or three trips I learned all the angles—there are always ways to make an extra dollar—and long ago I decided that I was my own best friend. In this business it's dog eat dog. In other words, these workers will take everything you can and will give them, and the more you give them the more they think they should have.

"So I have actually been forced to become a hard-hearted b——d in order to survive. I know all about the reformers and welfare people who criticize crew chiefs [he always uses the term *crew chief* rather than *leader* in referring to himself] like me. They come around every once in a while, talk to my people, and make trouble. Not very often do they bother to listen to my side. You want to? O.K., shoot with the questions. I got nothing to hide."

Like his crew members, Mr. Montero is a native-born Mexican-American whose base of operations is a medium-sized town in southern Texas, where he was interviewed on tape. He had just returned from a five months' trip in the northwest branch of the Stream, taking two busloads of ninety workers to Colorado, Oregon, and Washington, accompanied by two medium-sized auto trailers filled with baggage and household goods, one for each busload. Almost two thousand miles were clocked on the journey. All the arrangements and contracts were made and confirmed in advance—he is a good and experienced planner who knows the ropes—and "things moved like clockwork," the only setback being a delay in the ripening of one of the crops. Mr. Montero easily located another grower by telephone, and missed only a half day of work.

His employees usually worked together in the same fields, but sometimes they were scattered into as many as four farms in the same limited area, none more than five miles apart. One of his rules is that all members of a family work together, because, as he says, "they like it better that way."

Through the years he has established an ever-increasing number of regulations, necessary for him to "control them and never for a moment let them forget who is their *patron*. You have to keep them under control, just like little children; the minute you let go and show too much sympathy you are lost. The word goes around that you are an easy mark, and that can be the end of any discipline."

He always refers to his crew as "my people," not, however, with pride but rather to remind the listener of his responsibility. He used a good many swear words and highly uncomplimentary and vulgar descriptive adjectives and nouns which have been omitted. It is enough to note that he has little or no respect for them as people and human beings; he is, indeed, a modern counterpart of the slave-overseer of the past.

José Montero finished high school, with no further education except a correspondence course in bookkeeping to enable him to keep records. "Ninety people on the payroll means a lot of work, and everything has to be written down so there will be no arguments." He takes an adding machine on his trips and sets up his office in a central spot on each farm, preferably in the grower's office. "This makes it more businesslike," he says, "because my people take a deep breath before they come to see me."

He naturally exhibits complete self-confidence. Physically, he is short and stocky and dark of complexion, with

small beady eyes which never look directly at the person
to whom he is speaking. He constantly has an unlighted and
chewed cigar in his mouth, removing it from time to time.
He dresses somewhat flashily; never does he wear sloppy
work clothes because, he says, it would give an impression
that he was "equal with my people. No, I always have to
be the *patron;* it saves a lot of time because they don't
bother me as much as they might otherwise." He drives a
1965 Cadillac "to make a good impression" and has a large
house trailer with one worker to drive and take care of
him. There is no doubt at all that he is the boss. He insists
that his crew members address him as "sir" at all times.

Mr. Montero realized that the purpose of the interview
as explained to him was to obtain a picture of the methods
of a financially successful crew leader. On the promise that
his name would not be used, he said he welcomed the opportunity to tell of the difficulties a chief encounters. He covered a wide variety of subjects with only occasional prompt-
ing.

Here is the story in his own unedited words. He speaks
easily, in good English which he says he developed because
he deals with so many "big shots," his clients, and he adds,
"You have to make a good impression by knowing what
you are talking about."

I started this hauling business by investing in a pickup truck
on which I made a down payment, and did so well on the first
trip that I was able to pay for it complete from what I cleared.
I only had twelve people on that trip, but my profit was over
two thousand dollars. Now it is about twenty thousand each
trip, and I add to it by using the buses during the winter in
Texas [for both day- and long-haul work].

These buses you see I bought three years ago, and they are
in good shape, comfortable but hard to keep clean because my

people are not careful. It is quite a problem. I always have to repair some seats after each trip. My two drivers work for me all year; they are cleared by the authorities, and the buses meet the required standards. I don't want to have no trouble, so I go for inspection, otherwise they might come after me.

I am a good labor contractor. I have learned through the years how to strike a good bargain and get good jobs. The main thing is to make an agreement and live up to it. I used to work through the government office for everything, but now I have worked for so many growers that I know by the time I come back to Texas just about what my schedule will be for the next trip. This is because they know they will get fine work from my people—or else!

I have found that it is a good idea to contract for only one or two crops on each trip, like this time it was tomatoes and dry onions. I like to have my people do only field work. If they pick fruits ["ladder" work], they find out it is easier and they get unhappy and don't want to go into the fields anymore. Of course, it is dirtier, too, but my people don't seem to mind, especially if they expect to clear much money to bring back. If they complain it does them no good. I say, "Well, you can go back home, but how are you going to get there?" Besides, they are under contract to me, and they know I can blackball them and they will never work again if they quit. Of course, half my people are married, and about half of these have children, so they can do nothing.

These people have to be watched carefully, because they are very lazy if you let them be. They are also sneaky; they will not own up their debts to me, and will sometimes argue. But I always have everything written down, so in the end they accept my decisions. Most of the arguments are over money. I am paid an overall amount by the grower, agreed upon in my contract, and I pay for my people's rent and food and some other expenses. I make loans with good interest because if they need money besides their pay they have to come to me. They get little cardboard tickets when they turn in a full basket in the fields. There is an agreed rate of pay. I have a record of these, and at the end of the week on payday they give them to me and I have also notes of the expenses I have paid for them. I show them the adding-machine tape, so there should be no arguments. I pay them what is left over after these expenses are deducted. Sometimes they will try to argue, but there it is. They are never any good at arithmetic and they don't see where the money went; I have often thought it would be better to give them their full payment and let them worry about the rest, but it wouldn't work.

I have some trouble with winos and gamblers. Most of my people have no sense about money, and when it is gone they don't see where it all went, and they want an advance. This could easily get out of hand, so I charge 20 percent interest, and they pay it, believe you me. Part of this high charge is to keep them from throwing away their money. There is no use in reminding them that they should hold some of their money to take back home, or why would they go hundreds of miles away to work? But if they are not responsible, what's it to me?

Of course, I am a businessman, and my idea is to make a good thing out of the harvest seasons. I cannot afford to be too much of an easy mark because it would always cost. Naturally I have a few deals. Sometimes a grocer near the labor camp gives me a rake-off for all the stuff my people buy from him. (These are the families who cook in their houses.) Some crew chiefs get a concession from the grocer to sell sandwiches and soft drinks near the fields, but this is too much trouble for me. Some take their wives with them to run a store, but my missus stays home. There are all sorts of ways to make an extra buck, and these people are my income.

You want to know what I do about housing and such things as health and schools for the children? Well, we run into all kinds of different housing, generally barracks [dormitories] for the single men and separate houses for the families, sometimes two to a house. Sometimes they are pretty bad. It depends entirely on the grower. I have nothing to do with it. There are rules [standards] but it is not up to me to be sure that they are followed. If someone complains and I see things are really bad, I might talk to the grower, but if he doesn't want to do anything it's nothing to me. You see, they are only used during the harvest times when lots of workers are needed, and I can understand why a farmer will not want to sink a lot of money in such things. Some of my people think I am God and can change everything, but I tell them they can't expect too much and soon they will be going somewhere else where things will be better. This quiets them down. The average is pretty good, though.

Health? Yes, that's my responsibility. Healthy and happy workers are good workers. If they can't work they are no good to me, and so I try to get them well as soon as possible by taking them to a doctor or a clinic. This is so they won't waste time being sick and absent from the field. I pay the fees, if there are any, and deduct the bill from their pay. Most illnesses are like the flu; someone catches a cold from the dampness or a bug and is laid up. Some get the runs [diarrhea] from the food they eat and the water they drink; that is one of the commonest sicknesses. Sometimes they play sick and pretend that they can't work. This is when they are tired and just don't feel like going into the fields. Some are just plain lazy. They forget that it's no work, no pay, and you would be surprised how quickly they get well when I remind them!

The children? Well, they are supposed to work, that's part of my deal, and I don't allow any children under nine to come along. There is always some lighter work for them to do. I like to have them work because otherwise they are alone in the camp or some women stay away from the fields to take care of them. School? Never. They can go at home. This going to school for a short time is no good anyway because we are not in one place long enough—the longest stay was three to four weeks—and the kids are with strangers and the classes are hard to follow. Altogether it is better that they work, much less trouble that way.

The towns? Well, I tote my people in on weekends. They like to get a change. Sometimes there are dances and movies and entertainments. I get them back to camp by midnight; that is a rule. Some of the men go to bars and drink too much and spend their money. So I have wine for sale in the camp. They pay a dollar a pint—it costs me about forty-five cents—so there is a good profit in it.

Now, you should know something about these people. They will do no more work than they have to, and they will try to get away with anything I let them. So strict control is necessary. It is not that I am mean, but they need to be watched. Some of them are dirty and make a mess of their places, but they are probably the same way at home.

The family men are best, because they know they have to earn. The single men don't seem to give a damn; even if they have a family back in Texas, they seem to forget it mostly. Of course, some send money back home regular; in that way they know there will be some profit from their work.

How much do my people have after the trip? I don't pay much attention to it. But I would say that the singles have about three or four hundred dollars if they have been careful. The families, of course, take back more, the amount depending on how much work they do, how many work and how often and long the wives and children work. I would imagine the average is about five to seven hundred dollars, though some of the best and most careful may go as high as a thousand or twelve hundred dollars. All I know is what is on my records. I keep a separate record for each family, and I can therefore know whether they are doing well for me. This helps me to decide whether I will take them on the next trip.

I sign up my best people before they leave me. This is not written down because in the early spring I get in touch with them to be sure they want to go. They know that I stick to my promises.

There is always a turnover. Some workers are dissatisfied with the pay or the work, and they decide not to go with me again. The turnover? Well, I would say about a third do not want to go again, so I have to replace them. Some will go for two, three years and then quit. I have about a third who always go, they have been with me five or more years. They are the ones I can count on not to make trouble, because they know what to expect.

Yes, the business is good. One of these days I will retire. Probably I will sell my buses and give my workers to someone who wants to take over as crew leader, with a nice commission for me to live on. Or I will make a deal for someone to go on the trip for me, paying him a salary. Of course he will go with me first so he can become familiar with everything.

Exactly how many crew leaders there are like José Montero is impossible to determine, but his like occurs all too often. The federal (and in some cases the state) regulations may catch up with him, but workers hesitate to file complaints, so little evidence is available. A crew leader can always deny the allegations on the basis of the worker's "prejudice." Seasonal migrant workers hesitate to make complaints as a group, and do not employ the union tactics of strength in numbers. Their livelihood is at stake, and being labeled as "troublemakers" means that future employment is impossible.

It goes without saying that such exploiters disregard all the laws that have been enacted for the protection of workers. Anyone who dares to inquire about them is thoroughly rebuffed. Several state agencies have already reported extreme frustration in their attempts to check up on compliance with the new federal and state laws. Dependent as they are upon the crew leader, growers invariably do not concern themselves with the problems of his workers.

This type of labor contractor cares little about his crew members as human beings. In various studies, leaders have openly and frankly called them "animals, two-legged animals, beasts, destructive people, no-goods, shiftless ignoramuses, worthless 'spics' or 'niggers' " and the like. Aware of their basic fear of him, he knows how to "spank" them, as if they were children. Even Mike Bishop adopted this attitude.

As the employer of seasonal farm laborers, the chief possesses the power to make his charges happy, contented, and highly productive, or miserable, despondent, and subservient.

7

Profile of the Interstate Migrant

As we have already seen, a typical or prototype migrant farm worker is nonexistent. Migrant workers have only a few common characteristics: all travel from state to state, generally from south to north, harvest seasonal crops, follow the same work routines, and undergo somewhat identical experiences.

On the other hand, the differences are many. Migrant workers have varied backgrounds of race and dissimilar home bases from which they depart and to which they return. Their lives there have but one condition shared in common—poverty.

In their annual trips also, the variations are many. They may travel in groups under a crew leader or alone in their own automobiles. They may be experienced veterans of many journeys or inexperienced first-timers. They may cover one-way distances up to a thousand or more or only a few hundred miles. They may work several weeks in one locality or constantly move from place to place. They may work in a wide variety of field and orchard crops, or specialize in picking one or two vegetables or fruits. The differences could be multiplied almost indefinitely.

Even if one were to visit a labor camp and survey the occupants, the variations would be many and diverse. The answers to the questions: (1) who are the migrants? (2) what are their backgrounds? (3) what are their main characteristics as people? (4) where are the directions in their lives? (5) why do they travel to find work and make a living? can only be answered by individual migrants themselves, or by a social and psychological group study. The federal government has never attempted an overall study limited to the characteristics and lives of the total interstate migrant group.

However, a 1967 publication of the United States Department of Agriculture entitled *Domestic Migratory Workers: Personal and Economic Characteristics,* based on a survey made in December, 1965, deals with data obtained on 466,000 workers who left their home county to do farm labor as intrastate and interstate migrants. Of these, 139,-000, or about 30 percent, were interstate migrants who worked for wages in different states from their homes, and the information obtained offers some valuable insight.

Supplementing this single overall survey are several comprehensive studies undertaken in at least six states with large numbers of out-of-state farm workers: California (1961), Colorado (1961), Florida (1963), New Jersey (1966), Ohio (1961), and Oregon (1959). These have been made in order to obtain a better understanding of the problems faced by the annual visitors who make such a vital contribution to the states' economies.

From these studies, one can obtain insights that lead to an understanding of the migrant as a person. One must be aware that the information which follows has been obtained from special groups selected for questioning. However, they may be considered as representative, because the state studies quoted are designed to give as accurate a picture as is possible.

Contrary to general belief, the average interstate migrant is not young. An overall generalization would be that most, both men and women, are in their thirties. The wife is usually eight to ten years younger than her husband. The average ages given in the states studied are: Colorado, twenty to twenty-five for single men and thirty-five to forty for heads of families; for Florida, twenty to thirty-four for all; New York, thirty-two; and Oregon, thirty-six to forty for all.

Seasonal workers are predominantly male; the ratio of males to females (almost all wives) varies in the state studies. In California and Colorado it was three to one. In Florida the ratio was reversed, 81 males to each 100 females, undoubtedly because more men are accompanied by their wives, and daughters are more numerous than sons. In Oregon, males outnumber females ten to two, probably because of the distance of the state from the migrant's home base.

The number of children under sixteen in a traveling migrant family varies considerably. One was the number in both California and Colorado, in Florida from three to five, and in Oregon, where 80 percent of the working families had children accompanying them, the average was four. In the government study, 140,000 children in 32,000 families traveled with their parents. Interstate workers, particularly Mexican-Americans, were more apt to take their small children with them than were those who worked closer to their home bases. The families in the case studies in Chapters 2–4 had brought an average of two children with them on the trips.

Two state studies reported the number of years the migrants had been on annual trips. In Colorado, eight to nine years was the average; in Florida, the average was four years, but for many it was only a year. Suffice it to say that a large number are veterans. As one worker put it, "it gets to be a habit, and we jes' naturally decide to go again, hoping for better luck next time."

The length of stay in one place seems to depend upon the arrangements and contracts for the work. If the workers are there under a crew leader, he makes the decision. If he does not want to move over long distances, he will seek contracts within a somewhat limited area. Even if the journeys are as long as four months, the average, the crew might spend the entire time in one state, and often in one region of that state.

If a crew picks only one or two crops, they will probably travel longer distances because a short harvest period means they will have to go farther north for the later harvest of the same crop. In the Colorado study, by far the largest number stayed one month or less in a single place of work. Of the workers interviewed for this book, the longest work period in the same place was eight weeks. Most of the laborers worked in from four to six localities during the four-month trips.

Loners or families traveling alone and finding their own work must adjust the length of their stay in each place to the work they find. As a result, they are apt to work for a short period and then move on to wherever the next job is available.

Most interesting and revealing are the answers to the question "Why did you become a migratory worker?" Almost all answers cite identical reasons. The Florida study, for example, lists four reasons (presented here in the order of importance and frequency given): (1) loss of farm jobs, (2) no work in the local community, (3) did not like their home town and wanted to get away from it, and (4) wanted to be able to earn a good living. The Colorado study likewise cited four reasons: (1) that they would be unemployed unless they did seasonal farm work, (2) they had no other job skills, (3) they could make more money than in any other work, and (4) they enjoy it.

A Negro in New Jersey said, "It's better livin' than I had."

A Negro father following the Atlantic Coast Stream: "We wants a change and we willin' to take the chances. Our boss-man is good, an' he give us chance to take back 'nuff moneys so's we don't starve in de winters."

A white teen-age loner in the East: "Life in my home town is not lively. Nuthin' ever happens. I think maybe I like to go far away and see new people."

A southern Negro: "Law me, wu'nt nothin' else to do. Lan' all done 'cep' for eatin', none for sellin'. Cotton chop no good 'cep' certain times and long aways. Anythin' better than be there."

A young Mexican-American: "Not enough work for us at home. They don't want us Mexicans if they can get whites, and if we do work they treat us like dirt. I thought maybe strangers would be nicer if I had a chance to work for them."

Another Mexican-American: "All me and my *esposa* [wife] and *muchachos* [children] know is to work in the dirt. Nothing else we can do, but we *can* pick."

It goes without saying that migrant workers are currently paid far less than the United States standard minimum wage, which is $1.40 per hour, raised to $1.60 early in 1968, and that their annual income is far less than the minimum defining the poverty level ($3,300 for a family of four). Workers in industry enjoy the highest wage level of all laborers. Part of this is due to the efforts of labor unions. But all agricultural workers have been excluded from the federal legislation protecting labor, and the attempts to unionize them have been fought for many years, largely because of the opposition of the corporate growers. These have been able to resist the few attempts made by union organizers in behalf of both permanent and seasonal workers.

The beginnings of such efforts have been made in California, the largest user of farm labor in the United States. A landmark was achieved there in 1966, after an eleven-month strike of vineyard workers in 1965, accompanied by a nationwide boycott, against the Di Giorgio Corporation and Schenley Industries.

The demands were not only for an increase in the hourly wage (from $1.20 to $1.40), but for a higher payment incentive for piece-work (a bonus given to increase the amount of grapes picked) from fifteen to twenty-five cents a box (crate). The demands additionally covered many of the conditions of life and work such as housing, drinking water, and toilets. The strike campaign of marches and picketing, accompanied by extensive violence, was conducted under the leadership of Cesar Chavez, a Mexican-American who was the director of the AFL-CIO United Farm Workers Organizing Committee. He became a figure of national prominence during the strike in Delano. The significance of the 1966 victory was that the plight of migrant workers was brought again to the attention of the country. Until this time, the migrants by their very nature had neither cohesion nor leadership. The campaign is continuing; in early 1968, Mr. Chavez went on a fifteen-day hunger strike to publicize the cause, and during the summer, nationwide consumer boycotts of California grapes were in effect.

During the summer of 1968, New Jersey became the first state to recognize the right of migrant farm workers to unionize, when the Governor's Task Force on Migrant Farm Labor recommended the creation of a new state agency for the purpose.

Migrant farm workers are undoubtedly the poorest group of the employed in the United States. A contributing factor to their low annual and daily earnings is the very inferior prevailing wage rate in agriculture. Daily farm earnings of migrants averaged around ten dollars in 1965. In contrast, industrial workers earned about twenty dollars for an eight-hour day, or twice the daily wage of the migratory worker. The average annual income of migrants, computed in the government study already discussed, was about one thousand dollars. The average income of all workers in the United States in 1965 was $3,700, more than double the annual income of the highest income group of migratory workers, those employed at both farm and nonfarm jobs.

William Scholes, who has worked in the Migrant Ministry of the National Council of Churches, has pointed out that even if a worker was able to earn $1.25 an hour, the top pay in most areas of the country, his weekly income (ten hours per day, five days a week) would be $62.50 before deductions. But the migrant's schedule is often disrupted by rains and the extent of the harvest.

An average work year is about thirty weeks. This would produce an annual income of $1,875 per year, about 37 percent below the poverty level. Farm workers are not covered by hour and wage laws, and they are ineligible for unemployment insurance.

A few of the 1966 picking rates will serve to indicate

the overall picture: a head of lettuce, 1 1/3 cents; a pound of celery, 1/2 cent; and a grapefruit, 2/5 of a cent. In Colorado (1961) the overall hourly rate for migrant work was from seventy-five to ninety cents per hour. Much of the pay is based on quantity—box, pound, carton, or pail. For some vegetables the pay is woefully low, as revealed in the testimony of workers interviewed in the case studies in Chapters 2–4.

Few standard rates exist, many depend on the whims of the growers and the bargaining of labor contractors. Stoop labor is the most menial of all work, and this is reflected in the wages paid.

Seasonal migrant workers are in every way second-class citizens. Their way of life is rootless, and they are in bondage to poverty. Yet, driven by the hope that they will gain a better life, they doggedly continue their lives "on the season." As a Negro worker from Georgia expressed it, "I been everywhere and I got nowhere."

The interviews with migrants working in the three streams, forming Chapters 2–4, serve to reveal more personal aspects of their characteristics and lives. As may be seen, they were all facing specific and individual problems in their work and way of life during the 1967 trip.

The subjects for the tape recordings were selected on the spot, several on the recommendation of a crew leader as being interesting in a particular way and fairly typical of work they performed. Each was asked much the same questions designed to bring out the worker's (or workers') background, reasons for migrating on the season, achievements and disappointments, types of work, difficulties and unpleasantness encountered, and adjustment to the work.

Each subject was briefed on the purpose of the interview

and the information desired, and each was given the opportunity to become accustomed to talking into a recorder. None had ever before seen such a machine, much less talked while one was in operation. All were cooperative and apparently honest. Some were talkative, others timid, self-conscious, and uncommunicative even when encouraged and prompted. But all revealed the degradation they felt.

One of the difficulties encountered was to extract information and comments from those who were working and living under intolerable conditions with an insensitive crew leader. Not only were they hesitant to talk, for fear of reprisals, but their feelings of hopelessness were difficult to express. The freewheelers, set adrift and battling for enough work to sustain them, were usually unable to put their desperation into words. As a result, an impression may be conveyed that migrant workers in general are happy and fairly contented with their lot. The truth is exactly the opposite.

Most of the migrants interviewed had been on five or more annual trips. As one put it, "it gets to be a habit, and we jes' naturally decide to go again, hoping for better luck next time." Apparently this continuing hope never wanes in spite of their treatment, the physically tortuous work, and the privations of life on the season. The migrant life has become their way of life.

8

The Home
Away from Home

In September, 1967, the late Senator Robert F. Kennedy of New York, an active member of the Subcommittee on Migratory Labor of the Senate Committee on Labor and Public Welfare, visited several migrant camps in upstate New York with his fellow senator Jacob Javits. For several years the Subcommittee had been active in considering federal legislation to improve the plight of migrant workers throughout the country. Senator Kennedy had attended local hearings from coast to coast since 1965, and had visited many localities in California and the South, including Delano, California, and the lower Rio Grande Valley of Texas during the strikes of 1966. As a result, he was thoroughly familiar with the scandalous conditions under which many migrants live. But he hardly expected that they would be duplicated in his own state.

On this trip in their home state, the Senators were shocked by what they saw. At one farm they found a row of discarded buses that had been converted by the owner ten years earlier into living quarters for migrants. The seats had been removed and in them were filthy mattresses, windows covered with cardboard and wood, greasy stoves, and one light bulb. Running water was at a spigot outside, and an outhouse was nearby. Senator Kennedy told the farmer, "You are something out of the nineteenth century. I wouldn't put an animal in those things." Senator Javits said the buses were "horrible and as bad as anything I've seen." Senator Kennedy agreed: "It's as deplorable, dilapidated, disgraceful housing as I've seen anywhere in the United States. . . ."

At another farm, sixty-six women and children and thirty-eight men were living in twelve wooden shacks. The men had one shower stall and the women two, but according to the migrants, there had been no hot water for at least three weeks. The Senators summarized their impressions by agreeing that the conditions were "appalling and disgraceful," and urged stricter compliance with the state's sanitary code.

Several months later, Senator Kennedy declared, "The housing here is as bad as it is in Mississippi or Alabama or Georgia or California or in any other area in the United States that I have seen and inspected. We should lead the way here in New York."

The conditions observed by the Senators were the more shocking to them because New York state, the fourth largest employer of migrant workers in the United States in 1966, was supposedly active in its supervision and control of camps as a part of an overall program considered a model of its kind.

All too often migrants live like animals in inferior quarters, even in states which have shown consideration for them. In spite of stringent laws, this is one of the most unhappy features of their generally sordid lives.

Observers of migrant life unanimously agree that its most important aspects are housing and sanitation. These are important to the worker and his family, the farmer ("good worker housing is good farm business," according to the United States Department of Labor), the community where he makes his home for even a short time, and, eventually, the consumer who eats what has been harvested.

Housing is generally provided on or near the farm where the migrant works. Large companies, the corporate farmers, often operate a central housing complex in the work area. On other farms, workers may be sheltered in individual houses, multiple family units, barracks or dormitories (called "bullpens") for single male workers, cabins, shacks, and temporary shelters such as tents, trailers, abandoned trolley cars or buses, and the like. Adequate space is rare; families of five or six members are provided with one all-purpose room. Bedding, beds, window screens, cooking facilities, and plumbing are all too often lacking or of inferior quality.

Sanitary conditions are considered so important that regulations are often included as a part of housing codes or vice versa. Surveys have revealed that dilapidated outside privies occur most frequently. Often located close to unprotected water supplies, they are a source of contamination that leads to frequent outbreaks of disease. Chemical portable toilets are frequently not provided near the fields. Bathing facilities are generally poor, and water for bathing and cooking is substandard; hot water from the tap is often unavailable. Facilities for garbage disposal are inadequate, and roaches and flies abound, window screens are not provided, and the interiors are never or infrequently cleaned by the growers.

At a hearing of the United States Senate Subcommittee on Migratory Labor in 1965, the following conditions were cited as typical of most migrant camps throughout the country: ". . . the lack of proper toilets and water supply facilities is not the only health and safety hazard connected with migrant housing. Improper disposal of sewage wastes and garbage, leaking roofs, cracks in walls and floors which permit wind and dirt to blow into living quarters, lack of refrigeration, makeshift heating and cooking facilities, severe overcrowding, and infestation by rats and insects are other basic sanitation and structural housing deficiencies which contribute to poor physical, mental, and social health in many migrant camps. They lead to recurring colds, ear infections, accidents, burns, food poisoning or infections, poor diet, and juvenile and adult delinquency."

Laws, regulations, and codes covering housing and sanitation currently in effect in twenty-eight states require official approval of facilities to operate a camp. Local enforcement is generally weak, however, because of an insufficient number of inspectors, and many camps are visited only once or twice during an entire season. In attempting to attract workers and encourage their performance ("a happy worker is a good worker"), several states have offered and continue to offer assistance to growers. Under the Housing Act of 1961 and its 1964 amendments and the antipoverty legislation, the federal government is empowered to make direct grants and loans (see later discussions) to farmers.

Interest in minimum state and federal regulations was first encouraged by standards developed by the President's Committee on Migratory Labor in 1956. Revisions were made by the United States Department of Labor in 1967, making the Committee's minimum standards applicable to all employers of seasonal labor who wish to make use of federal assistance in recruitment.

State and federal laws and regulations prove ineffective, however, if they are not strictly enforced by the responsible local authorities. Three circumstances militate against compliance with these regulations and laws: (1) public unconcern or ignorance, (2) lack of sufficient inspection personnel, and (3) the resistance of farmers and local bodies to making improvements. Too often growers and farmers consider these regulations unnecessary and impractical, and the expenditures for improvements burdensome and excessive. Why, they maintain, should they invest substantial sums for facilities which are to be used only infrequently during the short harvest season and remain unoccupied for the other months of the year? One grower, who had been ordered to improve his facilities, stated, "The home I live in could not meet those standards!"

Many farmers are quick to express sympathy with and understanding of the migrants' plight. As one expressed it, "We should do everything possible to make life a little less bad for the workers whose sweat we live on."

Nevertheless, many farmers continue to provide substandard housing. Because New Jersey has been a leader in enacting legislation for migrant welfare, the state's experiences may be cited as an example of the realities to be faced even when stringent laws exist. Similar conditions have been exposed in several other states during the past few years; this account of New Jersey's difficulties should not be construed as a condemnation of its superior overall program.

New Jersey's Migrant Labor Code, which applies to all migrant labor camps, is a model in its coverage; requirements are explicit, and any camp which does not conform is deemed a "public nuisance." If improvements have not been made after five days, the camp is closed. An alternative is a minimum fine of two hundred dollars. In the three years, 1963–1966, 125 camp operators were cited for hearings with penalties ranging up to six hundred dollars.

During 1966, about twenty-one thousand migrants, forty-five hundred of whom were southern Negro interstate migrants, were housed in the state's 1,777 camps. Yet many still lived in ramshackle, overcrowded huts and cabins that lacked indoor water or toilet facilities. From mid-1965 through 1966, a dozen state inspectors had found several thousand violations of the Code. Many were minor and readily corrected. The inspectors found it impossible to visit the large number of camps regularly. Many were inspected only once, at the beginning of the harvest season. Ten percent of the camps were never inspected during the 1967 summer months.

Tragedies had been occurring regularly; eight workers had died in four years in fires, explosions of gas tanks, and asphyxiation from heating appliances.

During 1967, several instances of flagrant noncompliance with the Code in New Jersey received national attention. By June, three thousand "No Trespassing" signs had been posted around labor camps throughout the state in a campaign by growers to keep civil rights and antipoverty workers from reaching Negro migrants who were living "in squalid conditions." Coincidentally, a Governor's Task Force issued a strongly worded report with recommendations for reforms. For example, the group found that 17 percent of drinking water in the camps visited was "grossly contaminated with typhoid, hepatitis, and bacillary dysentery." One of the members described migrant farm labor in the state as "a peonage system . . . for poor, uneducated persons who have become lost in a morass of helplessness."

In August, 1967, the Task Force publicly exposed unlawful conditions in several specific localities in South Jersey, indicating that the state's Code was not being enforced. In one camp, according to the statement: "One hundred thirty migrants were housed in accommodations for ninety; the privies had overflowed into the nearby water supply; and in one seven-foot rat-infested room six children slept in one bed." Some families were even living in converted chicken coops. The operators of eleven camps housing 250 migrants were subsequently ordered to correct conditions within five days. The many violations cited included "overcrowding; rat and roach infestation; dilapidated, unsanitary outhouses; holes in the roofs and walls; shacks that had no beds, chairs, or tables for their occupants; condemned shanties that were being lived in; no refrigeration; polluted or insufficient water supplies; and, in some cases, no garbage facilities."

Invoking the law, the state authorities imposed on the owners of ten of the camps involved the five-day deadline for the removal of violations. Nine farmers failed to comply; they sought to delay because the picking of the tomato crop would be completed within a week or ten days and workers would move on. They were brought into court, and fines of $200 each were assessed on eight, with threats of added fines of $500 if they failed to correct the violations.

Simultaneously, state inspectors staged a series of predawn surprise visits to five of the camps, and found that some farmers had corrected the conditions, but four had done nothing. Several of them used mechanical pickers to complete the tomato harvest, and the victimized workers were unemployed. Meanwhile, the Governor belatedly issued a plan of major reforms which were to be put into force before the 1968 out-of-state harvesters arrived. The Governor's Task Force issued a controversial final report in the summer of 1968 which was highly critical of the state's Department of Labor and Industry for its enforcement of the laws dealing with migrant labor and housing. It recommended that the Governor's office assume direct responsibility for the welfare of migrant farm workers.

These incidents served to reveal the all-too-common attitude of farmers and growers toward their workers. They maintained that the migrants were irresponsible and destructive. Charging that the major blame for the conditions of even the substandard housing available lay with the workers themselves, a grower stated, by way of excuse for not making improvements, "These people live the same way at home; you can't break somebody of doing something they have done all their lives."

The chief "troublemakers" seem to be single men, rather than workers who travel with their families. Abe Lee, the Negro who was interviewed at one of the camps involved (Chapter 2), talked about these "troublemakers."

They is these mens who 'long our same way. They does not always work in same farms. But when they is large crops ripe for pickin', these mens turn up in the rows.

They is bad nigguhs, and, suh, you knows we culluds doesn't like that word, so when I calls 'em that I means real true bad. They has no wifes and famblies, at least they says not, but I thinks some lies and that they has lef' their folkses down south mebbe 'cause it better for everyone. Some camps does not have houses for famblies, and these mens can bunk together and can travel in a bus and can swear and get drunk.

A group is 'bout thirty or more and they travels with a boss who is s'pose to take keer of them. No wonder they is bad to behave ('cuz he is bad, too). You said you read in paper that one he sold them little bottles wine for fifty cents. That is kerrekt; in the stores they is dollah or more but he give them a "rate." Mebbe he not mean be bad and make them ak bad. I think he want keep 'em happy and don' care 'cep' that they do good work for him.

By bad nigguh I mean real bad. They is noisy and they is drunk lots at night and they is gambling and they is many fights. Sometimes they house is near us fambly cabins so we know. Bes' thing is to stay apart; the fambly mens forbid theys childrens speak to 'em and if we ketches 'em stopping we might use the strap 'cause it very hard to keep childrens respekkable anyways.

When the peoples from state comes here they looks shock at the houses, 'cause the windows is broke, the insides is filth-full and the bosses have pay no 'tenshun. The famblies tries keep things nice, but these mens spoils everything, and the state people is shaking theys heads and making little noises. That is why the farmer wuz so mad in the papers which was read us. I not lie and say alls famblies is clean and neat but we does try at least. These mens doesn't try and says it is nobody's business what they does; if they does the work and does not complains, the other things is jes' private 'tween 'em.

These mens is like tramps. They does not save theys pay and they is always owing and is therefore working for nuthin' lotsa time. They ginerally goes theirs ways and we famblies goes ours.

A tragic aftermath of the 1967 summer occurred in November at one of the South Jersey camps which had been condemned by the state authorities. In October, the State Department of Labor and Industry had issued an ultimatum to the owners that they must construct new buildings by April 1, 1968, or face a two thousand dollar fine. Shortly after Thanksgiving, five children, aged seven, four, two, one, and seven months, were burned to death in a four-room shack while their mother was absent picking leeks in a nearby field. They were found in a nine-by-twelve-foot bedroom close to a coal stove that was still burning. On the charred floor was an overturned electric-heating unit.

New Jersey is not the only state where growers continually flout the laws in the hope of not being discovered. Other states with excellent legal requirements and safeguards have encountered abundant evidences of violation.

Even in California, regarded as advanced in its attention to migrant workers, conditions have been far from satisfactory in the past. A 1963 survey of the state Division of Housing contained this discouraging statement:

More than eighty percent of the farm worker families live in dwellings which violate standards of health, safety, and comfort; nearly sixty-five percent of the dwellings occupied by general field workers were dilapidated or deteriorated. Pit privies still serve thirty-three percent of the such dwellings, thirty percent had no bathing facilities and twenty-five percent lacked even a kitchen sink with running water.

Ten percent of all dwelling units had no water supply at all, and in one community, ninety percent of the dwelling units obtained their water supply by hauling it several miles in pails and milk cans.

Twenty-one percent of all dwelling units had no sewage facility and disposed of household wastes directly on the ground. Thirty percent obtained water from a private well which, in most all instances, was located on a small lot within a few feet of a septic tank, cesspool, or privy.

Deplorable conditions of migrant housing and sanitation in several other states received local and national attention during 1967. While the summer harvest season was at its peak, four of the biggest and "probably filthiest" camps on the Eastern Shore of Virginia were the subject of a series of articles in *The Washington Post,* which characterized them as "ramshackle, urine-soaked, garbage-strewn, insect-infested, and clearly in violation of state and federal laws." Following charges by Representative Joseph Resnick of New York that these were "among the worst in the nation," United States Department of Labor inspectors visited the camps, condemned them as unfit, and ruled them ineligible for the federal recruiting service that supplies most of the migrant workers.

Shortly after Senator Kennedy's inspection trip, New York State's migrant housing again received criticism. Almost five thousand interstate and seven thousand intrastate migrant laborers work in the state during the harvest season and are housed in more than a thousand camps. All camps with accommodations for more than five workers are subject to the regulations in Part XV, "Farm Labor Camps," of a 1954 (with later amendments) sanitary code. Permits to operate are issued by the Department of Health annually prior to the opening of the season, after inspections which are the responsibility of the State Police.

In a November broadcast aptly titled "It Ain't No Place to Live In," WMCA, a New York City radio station with several outlets throughout the state, revealed that the federal government had given the state $81,000 in 1958 to develop a code spelling out decent housing standards for transients, with special attention to be paid to migrant workers. In 1964 a new model housing code was completed, but this was rewritten with migrant housing deliberately dropped from it (it is not even mentioned) as a result of political pressure imposed by New York farmers through their various associations.

Governor Nelson Rockefeller maintained that the state's sanitary code covered migrant labor camps, and said, "It is covered by the health laws. It's not in the housing code because it doesn't belong there. It's under health regulations and it is a very strict code, far more strict than any other state, but it is enforced by local government." Later he maintained that because the migrants came from other states the problem is a federal one.

A 325-page report made by the New York State study group appointed to draw up the new housing code included a draft proposal for a section on migrant housing. It described violations of the sanitary code that the members had observed, and offered specific recommendations for the migrant section of the revised state housing code. This report was suppressed, and the suppression was also reported by radio station WMCA, after which the state Housing Commissioner called attention to the difficulty of enforcing the existing code, which is the responsibility of county health and labor departments. He pointed out that these officers are generally appointed, and in farm communities the farmers make the recommendations.

Belatedly, a bill setting up procedures for enforcing public health laws and the sanitary code at migrant labor camps was passed by the State Assembly in May, 1968. Health officers would be required, instead of merely permitted, to take action on violations. Penalties of up to $100 could be levied for each violation, and health officers could order a camp vacated in the case of extreme violations.

Conditions in Long Island's Suffolk County, where thirty-six hundred interstate migrants worked in 1966, were described in a 1967 late summer exposé as "complicity with a system of bondage." The reactions were similar to those in New Jersey. The County Commissioner of Labor outlined a proposal to substitute year-round county residents for the migrants, a suggestion which was deemed unfeasible by farmers' organizations because "no one would work for the wages we can pay." A nine-member panel is to explore solutions to the problem.

A sad footnote to Suffolk County's situation occurred in mid-January, 1968, when three adults died of smoke inhalation in a labor-camp fire which began in a kerosene space heater in one of the cubbyholes of the barracks-like building. The fifteen occupants were not migrant workers because the harvest season was over, but the owner had been brought to court in October on violations of the state sanitary code and was awaiting trial. Inadequate heating was among the violations found at the camp.

Such examples of flouting the law continue to occur in every state with, fortunately, decreasing frequency. As increased national attention is focused on the disgraceful conditions wherever found, public apathy should cease and be replaced by outrage leading to both better enforcement of existing laws and the enactment of remedial legislation.

The federal government has taken an increasing interest in the problem of migrant housing. The question of enforcement of government regulations by state agencies is complicated and controversial. In most cases they are considered as suggestions to supplement state codes and laws, for the federal-state relations do not make compliance mandatory. This question is discussed in some detail in Chapter 12.

The compliance of farmers and growers to the housing regulations of whatever source has varied. Excellent single- and multiple-family houses are abundant. Several agencies of the federal government (the departments of Labor, of Agriculture, and of Health, Education, and Welfare) have published model plans of all types and offer advisory assistance and financial loans to interested farmers. Many thousands of workers in states using seasonal farm labor occupy excellent temporary quarters ranging from solid concrete and cinder-block houses to well-constructed wooden units. Conscientious farmers are in more and more cases providing acceptable individual and group units which meet the standards.

Under the antipoverty program, the federal government's Farmers Home Administration is authorized to pay as an outright grant as much as two-thirds of the cost of camp improvement or the building of new quarters. The remaining one-third is financed by a long-term loan at 5 percent interest. Housing built by such funds must be maintained by the growers at federal standards, the rents charged must be reasonable, and records must be available for inspection. Such incentives, if taken advantage of by farmers, should prove a boon to migrant workers.

A landmark step in migrant housing was announced in April, 1968—the first of its kind to be built in Texas and the largest built by private enterprise in the country, with federal help from the Farmers Home Administration of the United States Department of Agriculture. All had previously been built with public housing funds and supervision. The near-million-dollar housing project of fourteen one-story and nine two-story cinder-block buildings containing 144 one-bedroom and forty-eight two-bedroom units was built by the Castro County (Texas) Agriculture Housing Association, Inc., a nonprofit organization set up by thirty-five county farmers and twenty-seven businessmen in Dimmitt, where it is located. All units have kitchens, inside toilets, baths, hot and cold running water, and modern heating. The facilities also include a full-time health clinic supported by federal funds. The migrants bring their own furnishings, such as cots and bedding, and they will pay from $12.50 to $15 a week, including utilities. The project will house nearly a thousand adults and children at the peak harvest time in midsummer.

If migrants are not to be treated as people, said Oscar Rose in the WMCA exposé, "then it is a mockery to say that our migrant farm workers have a right to life, liberty, and the pursuit of happiness. For the migrants are always on the edge of death in their tar-paper shacks, they are not really free to leave and, instead of happiness, we offer them despair."

9

The Welfare
of the Workers

"What has a man from all the toil and strain with
which he toils beneath the sun?"

ECCLESIASTES 2:22

The health of migrants is closely related to the housing provided for them. Workers must be in good physical condition
for the long hours of back-breaking stoop- and ladder-
picking. The adjective "healthy" might well be added to the
statement "A happy worker is a good worker." Unlike those
in other occupations, the migrant does not have hospitaliza-
tion, health, or accident insurance.

However, since the enactment of the Migrant Health Act
of 1962, health services and family health clinics have been
established through federal financial assistance in nearly a
hundred communities (as of January, 1967) through the
Public Health Service's Migrant Health Branch, and nine
million dollars was appropriated for the fiscal year ending
June 30, 1968, with successive increases promised through
1971.

For the first time, therefore, health care and treatment are widely available, and remarkable progress has been made. Pilot and demonstration projects, some of them established before the availability of federal aid, have been successfully carried on in (to mention only a few states) Arizona, California, Colorado, Florida, Idaho, Maryland, Michigan, Minnesota, New Jersey, New York, Oregon, Texas, and Washington.

Projects throughout the nation usually include such phases of health as physical examination, tests for diseases, vaccination and immunization, infant and children's diseases, prenatal care, dental service, and treatment of communicable diseases such as venereal infections and tuberculosis. Many clinics are open on certain evenings for family or individual consultation; if a migrant has no means of transportation, he may be picked up at the camp and returned there. Some limitation in hospital care, however, results from the high cost of nursing and surgery as well as residence restrictions.

Like other worker groups, seasonal workers have occupational health problems some of which require continuous medical treatment. The main ailments—poisoning of the body system, dermatitis, and respiratory infections—are caused by the pesticides (insect and weed killers) used in both sprays and fertilizers.

Agricultural work injuries are also relatively common. These include strains, sprains, dislocations, and hernias, as well as bruises, cuts, and fractures. All must (or should) receive medical attention. Workmen's compensation laws for agricultural laborers were available in only seventeen states in 1967, and temporary disability insurance in only one, California.

The health of children is a major interest of medical personnel working with migrants. Vitamin deficiencies are common, and excessive intake of starches and fats causes a dietary imbalance which affects their general health. Hookworm, stomach worm, and diarrhea occur with alarming frequency. The infant mortality rate is appallingly high; many mothers do not have the prenatal care which would produce healthy babies. Studies indicate that more than a third of the expectant mothers never visit a physician.

No migrant worker needing medical attention should be denied it. The success of the existing programs and the growing attention being paid to the health of seasonal workers give assurance that federal and state funds will be made increasingly available.

Far too many migrant workers are held in the bondage of poverty. However, those traveling with a conscientious and successful crew leader are almost assured of a financial return for a season's work. If by some chance they encounter financial difficulties, they can borrow from him against future earnings. Some experienced families traveling on their own earn at least enough to make the trip worthwhile.

The freewheelers who have no plan or program and must depend on a combination of luck and rumor to find work live precariously from day to day, paying out almost all they earn for the expenses of lodging, food, gasoline, and that bogey of all automobile travelers, car repairs. Bad weather resulting in no work, inability to locate field labor in the area where they find themselves or, perhaps, the illness of the parent or a child, can leave them destitute, desperate, and hungry.

The 1958 Governors' Conference recognized this problem and appointed a committee to study ways of assisting "stateless" migrants. They suggested a reciprocal agreement or compact among the states where interstate migrants are employed: the state which the migrant called "home" would reimburse the one which made welfare payments to him during his absence. As an alternative, they recommended federal legislation for repaying a state which gives financial aid to a nonresident worker. The difficulties of administering the first proposal, however, were insurmountable since the local relief loads, even at that time, were reported as excessive. The second proposal may eventually be enacted as a part of the many new laws under consideration.

Most states, counties, and towns—migrants never visit cities—have welfare assistance available to the unemployed or indigent; this is a fact of modern life. But, unfortunately, out-of-state seasonal workers are not usually eligible for public assistance benefits because they lack the necessary residence requirements. The United States Supreme Court is currently (1968) testing the validity of such a prerequisite. Even when no such requirement exists, local authorities are hesitant about using their funds for "strangers."

In some states, the relief load is already so great that there is simply not enough money to add temporary residents to the public welfare rolls, even when no residence requirement exists.

The case for aiding needy and stranded migrants is wholly defensible. Unlike many of the unemployed who receive local public assistance, the seasonal farm laborer possesses a work skill, however menial, and welcomes the chance to work if he can only find it. Common justice, not to mention humanity, should make possible for him the welfare assistance which is offered without objection to millions of other Americans.

The citizens of many localities near which the out-of-state seasonal migrants work commonly refer to them as the "strangers in our midst." Too often that is exactly what they are, and in more cases than not they remain anonymous.

The experiences of the temporary workers in the not-too-distant past have in the main been unhappy. Signs reading MIGRANTS NOT ADMITTED were sometimes posted on stores, eating places, and motion picture houses in communities near the camps. For the most part, local people avoided the migrants when possible, fearing they were dirty, disease-ridden, and prone to stealing. Townsfolk locked their doors when the migrants were in the vicinity, and were relieved when they were gone. Gradually, however, people in an increasing number of communities have begun to feel an obligation toward these strangers. After all, the work of the migrants is necessary to the local economy, bringing prosperity to the communities. Then, too, citizens have come to realize that, however strange they may seem, these migrants are human beings who deserve some of the advantages which each local citizen accepts unquestionably as a part of his life.

Some of the services which such enlightened communities are increasingly providing are health, day care, recreation, and schools. Most of these programs are made possible through state and federal financial support; only occasionally are local funds used. The participants in such plans —doctors, nurses, teachers, and social workers—are both paid and voluntary, and they give evidence of the fairly recent goodwill toward the visitors. Non-professional volunteers have played a part in the success of such programs.

Church groups were among the first to go into farm labor camps—not only to serve the spiritual needs of the migrants but also to bring other more practical services to them. They have organized volunteers and developed programs in a great many communities. In addition to conducting a program of activities, they also offer the human touch of friendship, concern, respect, and a desire to help. Migrants invariably respond with happiness and appreciation that someone cares.

Two national programs have taken the lead in such community action. The Migrant Ministry of the National Council of Churches (Protestant) pioneered in direct services to migrants in 1920 in three farm labor camps on the east coast. The work is now conducted in thirty-eight states, and in 1966 its services reached almost three hundred thousand seasonal workers. The paid staff was assisted by more than nine thousand volunteers. As far as is possible, every type of service is given. Catholic organizations have likewise been active. Their activities are on a parish basis, with diocesan support. The local priest is the key to success.

Such programs, supplementing those under local and state auspices, have led to increasing acceptance of migrants, and they are often welcomed in communities where plans have been carefully worked out in advance of their arrival. This includes welcoming parties and folk festivals, and giving them a feeling that they are a part of the community even for the relatively short time of their stay. Twenty-eight states now have committees which assist local groups in organization, plans, and programs.

Not really belonging to any community, the migrants have missed out on school, church, health, welfare, and recreational services. When they come to a community that is interested in them and tries to do something for them, they lose their feeling of strangeness. Once the contact has been made, the migrants genuinely look forward to their return during the next harvest season. The United States Department of Labor's interest in such programs is expressed in the slogan "Welcome, stranger!—Goodbye, friend."

Much has been accomplished through the Community Action Program of the Economic Opportunity Act of 1964 (the federal antipoverty bill). A section titled "Assistance for Migrant and Other Seasonally Employed Agricultural Employees and Their Families" authorizes, among other things, grants for community centers for migrants and the improvement of migrant-community relations, including health, recreation, education, and rest facilities. Both public agencies and private nonprofit organizations may apply, accompanying their request with specific proposals and plans for which the need must be justified. Up to 90 percent of the estimated cost is provided by the government. Several statewide, as well as county, programs are already in action.

In spite of the advances being made in cementing the relations between communities and their seasonal visitors, however, residents in many localities are still unconcerned. They refuse to accept the migrant as a person—a person generally belonging to a minority group, very different in background, often nearly or entirely illiterate, and disadvantaged.

Consider the following reactions, two from rural citizens in New Jersey and Colorado, and one from a crew leader who feels a threat to his hold over his charges.

A New Jersey woman expressed her attitude of suspicion and ingrained anti-Negro bias, with a justification for her lack of interest. "We have a few Negroes in our town," she said. "They do some of our work, and they live in their own part of town. But these Negroes from the South are different. They are not as well kept, and they talk funny;

sometimes you can hardly understand them. Besides, they are here for only a short time, and then they move on. Sometimes we hardly know they are around, because they keep to themselves. Of course we see figures in the fields, but they are not really people to us."

And a man in Colorado struck the same note in talking about the Mexican-Americans. "Up here we do not have any of these spicks [the derogatory term for persons of Spanish blood]," he said, "and they are so different that we just look at them when they are in town. Lots don't even bother to speak English, and most people hereabouts don't understand Spanish. Then too we can't help but be suspicious of them. It's really too bad, but I must confess that we are as prejudiced against them as we are with the niggers, and all the talk about mixing is just talk. I suppose you would say that it is on our consciences; maybe underneath we feel guilty because they have a helluva life, and the farmers just couldn't do without them."

And, finally, José Montero, the crew leader who does not consider his Mexican-American workers human beings, expressed his very strong feelings. "I don't want my people to mix with the people in the towns nearby," he began. "They really don't have the time for all that foolishness. When they get all the dances, parties, and such things put on especially for them, they always look for something more and they get out of hand. I am afraid some of these town people, the do-gooders, ask a lot of questions, and then my people start feeling sorry for themselves because of the way I treat them. They get too many ideas and start complaining and making trouble for me. In the South it isn't that way; most whites don't get on a personal basis with them, and therefore all is well. In the North there is all this talk about rights, and some of my people who were quite happy in the South decide that it is just plain heaven up North, and last year about five didn't even go back with me. They used the money I had made for them to start a new life; God only knows what they will work at, because they only know picking. Maybe it is the welfare they want. Ambition to get ahead? Well . . . yes, maybe, and from that idea I suppose they have a reason, but what can they do except the dirty work? Someone has to do it, you know."

10

The Plight
of the Children

"The most dramatic deprivation in migrant labor is
visited upon the children."
MICHAEL HARRINGTON, *The Other America*

Young children of preschool age, and those of school age
who are not permitted to work in localities where child
labor laws are enforced or where schools are unavailable,
constitute a unique problem. If, as is usual, the mother
works, she often takes them with her to the fields, checking
on them from time to time. Neither farmers nor crew leaders
like this practice. Or she may leave them in camp to be
cared for by an older child or a nonworking mother. Time
becomes a burden to them, and they eagerly await the
return of their parents.

To meet this situation, a large number of states and communities have established day-care centers which are in
operation during the working hours. Unlike other available
services that migrants ignore, child care is recognized by

146

the mothers as an important part of their lives since they must be free to accept work when it is available.

The pioneer programs of Florida and New York have proved to be particularly effective. In Florida, where the harvest season is winter, children of six to sixteen are required to be in school, but, with the parents working, the care of preschool children poses a problem. As yet, nursery schools throughout the state are operated only in large camps. In New York, centers or day nurseries for children from eight weeks to fourteen years of age are operated under contract by the New York State Federation of Growers and Processors. The state bears 90 percent of the cost with the remaining 10 percent paid by the growers and local migrant committees. A fee of fifteen cents per day per child is charged to the parents with a fifty-cent maximum regardless of the number of children enrolled in one family. A 1966 innovation was the hiring of migrant women from the camps for work in the centers. They are given on-the-job training and are paid $1.25 per hour. The centers program has been hailed as one of the bright spots in New York State's efforts on behalf of migrants.

Mrs. Mattie Lee (Chapter 2), on her 1967 trip, certainly appreciated the day-care center operating near the farm where she was picking cherries with her husband and two older children. "When we got there," she said, "lo and behold, they would not let my two babies [Eliza, twelve, and Charles, ' 'most' fourteen] work. It was the first time when anyone had objects [objections], but it was the law they told us about. Now, of course, they are both old enough to stay alone in the camp while we work, but I didn't like that. We heard about this place, and it didn't cost much. It was worth the money [thirty cents] a day just to know they were all right, and they had fun with other children

from several camps. They felt comfortable, too, because
'most everyone was colored, too.

"They played outdoors and in, read, sang, and did art
[crafts]; here is a weaving Eliza made. She also sewed some
of the clothes I sent with her, and she even tried to cook
—nothing fancy, but she will catch on. They had good and
reg'lar meals, and snacks, too. The nice thing for Abe and
me was that no matter how early we were off to work—we
had to go an hour's ride for two weeks and started at five
in the morning—the children were took care of, and they
stayed until we were back, sometimes long after dark.
[The centers open at six and close as late as nine, depending on the crops and the weather.] It gave them some rest
which they deserved because they worked six days a week
on the way up. Bless them nice people, they sure helped
my burden."

Funds for this most pressing problem of migrant families
are available under the provisions of the Economic Opportunity Act of 1964, and the pilot projects approved thus
far (1968), both statewide and local, have demonstrated
their value and effectiveness. For example, in its first year,
federal funds in New York totaled $171,000 to be added
to the state's $92,000, and the day-care program was en-
larged by the addition of ten centers.

The children in migrant families have been characterized
as the most educationally deprived in the nation. Most of
them enter school late, their attendance is poor, their
progress is slow, and they drop out early. Their unfortunate
plight has become a national problem, since illiteracy and
the lack of even an elementary education can cause a life
of uselessness and poverty.

Their average years of schooling are seven as compared

with the national average of ten. A New Jersey study in 1966 reported that as few as one in twenty enters high school. Attendance of the migrant child is constantly interrupted by the movement of his parents from one locality to another. Each time a move is made he loses time from classes. Very soon he becomes almost hopelessly behind in his schoolwork and unable to keep up with his ever-strange and new fellow pupils. The schools he attends often cannot meet his problems. Placing him in the proper grade is difficult if not impossible, without knowledge of his academic background. The United States Office of Education has developed a transfer record system to overcome this obstacle, but it has not been uniformly used. The provision of extra teachers to care for the seasonal influx of migrants is difficult. Unless summer schools are provided, a migrant child may attend only in May and a part of June, and will miss the first few weeks, and sometimes more, of the fall term.

Surveys reveal that about 50 percent of all children "on the season" never enroll in school. There are several reasons: the parents' need for the children's earnings or for older children to care for the younger brothers and sisters while the mother works in the field, the language barrier of those who speak only Spanish, and the difficulties in integration for Negro children. Some communities are indifferent to migrants, in others the attendance laws bar transients. Many children lack the proper clothing to make them comfortable.

Much has been accomplished in some localities, however. Special school programs have been set up in several states when the migrant population is largest, mainly in summer, and an increasing number of communities have established their own short-term programs.

An encouraging trend is the granting of federal anti-poverty funds through the Office of Economic Opportunity, under the Economic Opportunity Act of 1964, to school systems along the migrants' routes. These provide for special remedial instruction, food, clothing, and school supplies. A growing number of workshops for teachers of migrant children are being conducted in various parts of the country.

New Jersey is an example. Always a pacesetter in its attention to migrants, the state obtained one million dollars for its total Migrant Opportunity Program under the anti-poverty act. One of the features was a seven-week remedial and elementary education program conducted in seven schools for four hundred migrant children. Two children in the Lee family (Chapter 2) attended one of these schools in south New Jersey. Their mother praised the program.

"My eight-year-old boy and ten-year-old girl can't always work. They just plain gets too tire. They miss lots of school when they is away with us so long. So when Mister Bishop said there was this school not far away, we jumped to it. They are far behind, but here they gits speshul learning. Jonah, the boy, likes reading but he has trouble, and first thing I know he is bringing home books in the evening for to read. They have no books to take away in Gawgia. He gets so interested I have to take the book away 'less he not eat. He even wants to read late and keep the light on. He have a word book [dictionary] and he stops reading and turns the page to find the words. It is very different from home. My girl Jane likes the science—water, bugs, animals, volcanics, and such—and she is just as bad. The books are nicer than down South, big letters, pitchers, and such. Glory, I don't know what do with them now!"

In the fall of 1967, under a federal grant, California schools began teaching Mexican-American children in Spanish, with English taught as a second language until the third or fourth grade. This is expected not only to help the migrant children (ever present because of the continuous harvests) to understand the subject matter better, but also to remove the psychological stigma of being made to feel that their own language is somehow "bad" and that because of it they are set apart from others.

Another federally financed pilot program, unique because it provides for continuance of schooling as the children move farther north to Delaware, New Jersey, and New York, was begun in eastern Virginia (the key Delmarva Peninsula) in 1966. The children, from ages seven to twelve, are selected by the crew leaders, who will also assist in the followup. For six weeks, while their parents and older brothers and sisters are at work picking beans, tomatoes, and cucumbers, 350 Negro (and a few Mexican-American) children are given basic instruction. Through a coordination system, the parents take the records with them for use at the future work localities.

Such programs help make up for the educational deprivations which are a part of the rootless migrant life.

11

Man Versus Machine

The threat of the machine is increasingly a fact of life for both the migrant farm laborer and the crew leader. Statistics on the replacement of workers vividly show the reason for this uneasiness. A New York State study of snap-bean harvesting discloses that a machine operating for an eight-hour day harvests an average of ten tons, while an efficient single picker working the same number of hours averages about three hundred pounds. A 1966 California state agricultural mechanization survey revealed that an onion harvester with an operating crew of twelve men replaces forty pickers; a blackberry harvester (with a crew of five) replaces forty or more; a sweet potato harvester (with a six-man crew) replaces twelve to fourteen workers and a two-man chili-pepper harvester, fifty. This study estimates that by 1980 about half the present farm jobs will have been eliminated by automation and mechanization.

Some of the crops which are currently being harvested by machines (some models are experimental, but most are currently available in the commercial market) are asparagus, beets, broccoli, Brussels sprouts, cantaloupes, carrots, chili peppers, corn, cucumbers, lemons, onions, oranges, peas, and potatoes (both white and sweet).

Shakers and catchers (fruit-tree pickers) are being used in orchards for the following: almonds, apricots, cherries, olives, peaches, plums, prunes, and walnuts. However, most fruits are delicate and must be picked by hand.

But two circumstances indicate that seasonal farm workers will never be completely replaced by machines. The first is the high cost of these complicated automatons, particularly until they are mass-produced. A snap-bean harvester, for example, is priced at about twelve thousand dollars, and an ordinary farmer would hesitate to invest that large a sum for the limited seasonal use he would make of it. Only the huge companies would consider such an investment both practical and warranted. In addition, the methods of cultivation often have to be completely changed if harvesting machines are to be used.

The second fact is that many vegetables and fruits which can be picked mechanically for canning must be hand-picked for markets. Uneven periods of ripeness may require several pickings in order to obtain the highest possible yield. The tenderness of some crops and the predictable time lag before they will reach the housewife necessitate hand-picking. Bruises on fruits cause immediate decay and perhaps complete loss, and their appearance makes them unsalable. Lettuce is a good example. The machines often bruise the outer protective leaves, which are further damaged and decayed in transit, resulting in a crushed appearance and a reduction in the size of the head. Then, finally, a good many vegetables and fruits must always be picked by hand. Artichokes, most berries, and certain varieties of tomatoes are examples, while practically all fruits are fatally bruised by machines. How increased mechanization will affect the migrant farm worker will undoubtedly be one of the economic problems of the future. If they are no longer needed in such large numbers as at present, where will they find work to sustain them? And what other skills might they develop to provide them with a livelihood?

12

A Fair Deal

"The migrant laborer is unorganized, doesn't vote, has no money and no voice to speak with in legislative halls. The migrant is by nature not in one place, is usually in the backwoods where affluent America doesn't see him. He is the annual exploited man of the year."

ARTHUR HARDWICK, JR.
New York State
Assemblyman

Migratory workers first became a significant source of seasonal labor supply during World War I, when manpower for farm work was limited. Some attention was paid to the problem of their children's education in the 1920's. California, which recognized its migrant problems earlier than other states, developed mobile schools, an experiment which unfortunately proved unsuccessful.

Not until the Depression of the 1930's (Chapter 1) was there substantial public recognition of the plight of the migrant; this was the time when the conditions of their lives and work were at their worst. This situation aroused the concern of many citizens particularly those in religious and welfare groups. Between 1936 and 1942, a number of congressional investigations were initiated, and federal agencies made some attempts to meet the problem. As a result of the hearings of the La Follette (Senate) and Tolan (House) Committees, President Franklin D. Roosevelt appointed an Interdepartmental Committee to Coordinate Health and Welfare Activities, which issued a report and recommendations for action.

World War II temporarily diverted attention from the issue. From 1937 to 1943, as part of the program to help farm families impoverished by the Depression, the Farm Security Administration of the United States Department of Agriculture developed a farm labor camp program (the Joads in *The Grapes of Wrath* stayed in several of these camps). After the war, the Department of Labor attacked the problem, specifically through its Bureau of Employment Security, which is still continuing its essential work (Chapter 5). Postwar activities increased, and emphasis was placed on child labor.

The President's Commission on Migratory Labor was created by an executive order of President Harry S Truman in 1950. Hearings at strategic localities throughout the country formed the basis of a 1951 report and recommendations, which included a comprehensive program for improving local conditions. This report is still being used as an aid in developing goals and current legislation and programs.

Another landmark was the work and report of the President's Committee on Migratory Labor, established by President Dwight Eisenhower in 1954. It called for a mobilization of various federal agencies in stimulating more effective programs and service for migrants and in providing services to state and local areas where they worked. This report also continues to form the basis for contemporary government activities.

As has been pointed out (Chapter 8), the federal regulations, recommendations, and even laws can be enforced only through the responsible state agencies. In varying degrees, states have enacted a mass of their own legislation, but enforcement is too often lax.

A basic assumption of federal regulations and laws, in whatever field, is that they are considered to be binding upon lesser governmental units, and obedience is intended to be compulsory, since they are the law of the land. For example, the federal regulations for the registration of crew leaders should be obeyed in states having no such statute, and should be considered as higher authority by those where migrant labor codes are in effect. In practice, however, the doctrine of state's rights implies that obedience is not required; the federal laws are too often considered as not binding upon lesser governmental units unless some penalty for noncompliance is specifically stated.

When money grants are involved, the government, holding the purse strings, is in a favorable position to outline definite requirements and demand compliance as one of the conditions of the grant. One of the weaknesses in our present mammoth antipoverty program is that checks on the use of funds, and adherence to the conditions of the awards, have too often been lax. Only when misuse has been exposed after the money has been spent have further grants been either reduced or discontinued.

Under an ideal system, state and local authorities should supervise the projects and expenditure, but here again enforcement by the bureaucracy is often either weak or nonexistent.

More recent legislation specifically defines the conditions

and controls and requirements, as in the case of the migrant program under the Economic Opportunity Act of 1964 (the antipoverty and Great Society legislation). Proposals must be detailed according to a required outline; funds will not be granted for a vague and undefined project.

To summarize, it may be said that in general the federal standards and regulations noted throughout this book are often regarded only as suggestions and recommendations to be made a part of, or to supplement, state codes and laws.

Sincere efforts continue on all levels of government. The 1960's have been marked by increasing concentration upon migrant farm labor. Committees of both houses of Congress—the Senate Subcommittee on Migratory Labor of its Committee on Labor and Public Welfare, and the Subcommittee on Migratory Farm Workers of its Committee on Interstate and Foreign Commerce, and the House Subcommittee on Labor of its Committee on Education and Labor and its Committee on Interstate and Foreign Commerce—regularly conduct hearings in Washington and in key localities throughout the nation. Tangible results have already been achieved in the enactment of basic legislation and proposals for new laws.

The key areas currently being emphasized are collective bargaining (Chapter 7), minimum wages, and the many labor aspects of the migrant's work; health care; housing; education; and child labor. The annual reports of the Senate Subcommittee on Migratory Labor (see Sources and Readings) describe the current developments and proposals for legislation, and form concrete evidence of continuing interest on the national level. Another indication of government concern is the inclusion of federal funds through grants-in-aid under various laws. These have been referred to in Chapters 8–10.

Individual states, particularly those where the productivity of agriculture depends in whole or in part upon the migrants' work, are devoting increased attention to the "strangers in our midst." States have laws and regulations on some phases which have not yet been included in the federal laws. What may prove to be a landmark in state cooperation was the establishment during the late summer of 1968 of a migrant interstate panel of thirteen Atlantic Coast states (plus Puerto Rico and the Bahamas) to push a stepped-up drive to solve the problems of migrant laborers.

Lacking permanent residence, seasonal farm workers cannot carry weight as a voting bloc, and their interests must be furthered by individuals and organizations of good will. All levels of government—federal, state, and local— must be continually reminded that this nonvocal minority is still confronted with work and life situations which are intolerable in our affluent society.

The Subcommittee on Migratory Labor of the United States Senate is in the forefront of federal efforts on behalf of the migrant worker. In his 1965 report, the chairman, Senator Harrison A. Williams, Jr., of New Jersey, made this statement:

In the five years since it was established in August of 1959, the Subcommittee has faced up to the fact that the migratory worker lives and works in conditions that must be recognized for what they are—a national disgrace.

Senator Williams cited several specific federal accomplishments: The Migrant Health Act of 1962, crew leader registration, and the inclusion of various elements of the migrant's life in the War on Poverty legislation (the Economic Opportunity Act of 1964): housing, sanitation, child day-care, and education. Even so, he acknowledged that much remained to be accomplished, stating

> Decades of neglect have left a stockpile of misery and deprivation. Our [federal] programs thus far offer anti-dotes for specific ailments in the migratory farmworker system, but root causes of misery remain almost untouched. . . .

The Senator then listed the following as "unfinished business": a minimum wage, collective-bargaining rights, unemployment insurance, consideration of the dangers involved in child labor, workmen's compensation, general welfare assistance without a residence requirement, and the right to vote (now denied migrants because of the residence requirements which conflict with his mobility).

Continued emphasis on the elimination of poverty by the government resulted in Senator Williams making the following statement, with immediate goals, in the foreword to the Committee's 1966 report:

> Americans are discovering that poverty cannot be fought solely with money and sporadic goodwill. Understanding is the major weapon against want. Until we really *know* what it means to be poor in a generally comfortable nation, we will have neither the sensitivity nor the staying power needed for final victory.
>
> The need for perceptiveness and receptiveness is especially great when we consider the problems and progress of migratory farm workers. Progress has thus far [as of January, 1966] been considerable, in dealing with long-standing, readily viable, and shocking deficiencies in educational, health, and housing resources.
>
> And some might say that we have finally made it

possible for the migrant to live in decency and dignity.

But Congress and the people of the United States have yet to face up to these major facts:

1) Migratory farm labor must have a minimum wage.
2) If we ever hope to have a stable citizen farmwork force, we must establish orderly procedures for recruitment and for collective bargaining.
3) We must provide other basic protections, such as workmen's compensation and more flexible residence requirements for public assistance.

Our farm labor system could soon become a credit to this nation instead of a nagging prod to our conscience. . . . What we need now is an aware public and a Congress determined to complete the job.

Senator Jacob Javits of New York, a member of the Subcommittee, has concisely pinpointed the special situation of our migrant farm workers:

Domestic migratory workers are a chronically low-income group which, because of factors inherent in agricultural production, has unique problems: limited and intermittent periods of employment, travel over great distances in search of work, and the lack of benefits which flow from continued year-round employment in one place.

Though progress has been made on behalf of these rootless people, particularly during the 1960's, much remains to be done. Strong laws must be passed and rigidly enforced. All persons of goodwill in our country will enthusiastically approve of any and all efforts which would free America's migrant workers from their status as second-class and neglected citizens.

Appendix I—Definitions of Terms

Agribusiness: large-scale farming on enormous farms and ranches owned by large corporations (as absentee landlords, groups of investors, or holding companies), which mainly produce those crops (cotton, vegetables, and fruits) requiring large quantities of seasonal labor. Such farms generally include packing and processing facilities near the fields and orchards.

Agricultural migrant: one who, performing short-term farm work and moving from one job to another during the harvest season, finds it necessary to reside away from his or her home base (United States Department of Agriculture official definition).

Braceros: Mexican farm workers who enter the United States under contract to do temporary, mostly seasonal, farm work. They were the chief source of foreign farm labor in our country from 1951 (under Public Law 78) to the termination of the program on December 31, 1964.

Contracts; *see* Crew leader; Labor contractor.

Corporate farming; *see* Agribusiness.

Crew; *see* Labor crew.

Crew leader: any person who, for a fee, recruits, solicits,

162

hires, furnishes, and transports ten or more migrant workers at any one time in any calendar year for interstate agricultural employment. The leader accompanies the crew which he has recruited on their travels (United States Department of Labor official definition). The term is also used for an organizer of local and intrastate workers; *see also* Labor contractor.

Day-haul: a local commuter program for transporting local workers daily to and from their farm jobs from designated pickup points; *see also* Day labor; Local worker.

Day labor: local workers recruited by means of local radio and television spot announcements, newspaper advertisements, and even by sound trucks or word-of-mouth advertising. Prospective workers are asked to report at carefully chosen pickup points, where they are interviewed and selected. Much of this recruiting is done in advance, as are arrangements for transportation; *see also* Day-haul; Local workers.

"Follow the sun": a phrase used by migrant workers to describe their movement northward from crop to crop and area to area to harvest the field and orchard crops at the peak of their ripeness; *see also* "On the season."

Foreign worker: one who is imported under contract from outside the boundaries of the United States to perform seasonal farm labor, generally harvest work, for varying periods of time; *see also* Braceros.

Freewheeler: an individual migrant farm laborer who travels with or without his family, rather than as a crew member, seeking seasonal work wherever he is able to find it; *see also* Single.

Gate-hire: the system of employing a farm worker (or workers) whose arrival has not been scheduled in advance; *see also* Walk-in.

Grower: the general name for all farmers, whether independent or corporate.

Imported labor; *see* Foreign worker.

Interstate migratory worker: a person who leaves his home temporarily to do farm work in another state or in other states (United States Department of Agriculture official definition).

Intrastate migratory worker: a person who lives in a particular state and travels to various sections within the state, sometimes merely from one county to another, or, more often, to localities far from the home base, with various periods of absence (United States Department of Agriculture official definition).

Labor contractor: an alternate name for crew leader, but which refers also to any grower, processor, canner, ginner, or packing-shed operator who engages in any such activity for the purpose of supplying migrant workers solely for his own operation (United States Department of Labor official definition); *see also* Crew leader.

Labor crew: a group of seasonal workers who travel together under a crew leader.

Local worker: a farm worker recruited in towns and cities near the farm where needed for the harvests at any time during the year. Farm workers may be men or women, or young people when schools are not in session, mainly the summer months when peak harvesting generally takes place; *see also* Day haul; Day labor.

Long haul: the transportation of intrastate and interstate farm workers for distances of various lengths from their home base; *see also* Day haul.

Migrant: *n.*: one that migrates, as a person who moves into another area in order to find work. Also *adj.* (*Webster's New International Dictionary,* Third Edition).

Migrant agricultural worker; *see* Agricultural migrant.

Migratory: *adj.*: a) moving habitually or occasionally from one region of climate to another; b) moving in response to the demand for seasonal labor (*Webster's New International Dictionary,* Third Edition).

Migratory worker: a person who leaves his home temporarily to do work for wages in another county or state; *see also* Agricultural migrant; Interstate migratory worker; Intrastate migratory worker.

"On the season": a phrase used by migrant workers to denote their activities in seasonal farm work; *see also* "Follow the sun."

Piece work (or rate): a method of payment by unit (box, carton, bag, basket, etc.) at a standard rate per unit, designed as an incentive to production.

Single: a male farm worker who travels without his family (if he has one) to perform seasonal farm work. He may be a member of a crew or may travel alone as a freewheeler; *see also* Freewheeler.

Supplementary farm workers: those who are needed to supply a large and fluctuating seasonal demand for labor. They are categorized as local and migrant, depending on their mobility (United States Department of Agriculture official definition).

Texicans: an alternate name for the native Americans of Mexican descent from Texas who work as intrastate or interstate migratory farm workers in the Central and Pacific Coast Streams.

Walk-in: a farm worker who arrives unscheduled at a field or orchard and is hired on the spot; *see also* Gate-hire.

Appendix II—Migrant Workers in the United States

The number of interstate seasonal migratory workers, the subject of this book, is difficult to arrive at because the statistics reported by the United States Department of Labor, admittedly incomplete, do not include loners and free-wheelers who wander singly or in groups from place to place without making contact with the federal and state employment offices which compile the census. Yet they number many thousands and would undoubtedly enlarge the official figures substantially.

The numbers of all types of farm workers during selected years from 1949 to 1965 are indicated in Table I.

Table II shows the number of intrastate and interstate migrants for the peak month of the year 1965 and the number of interstate migrants for the month of their peak employment. It should be noted that the latter figures (column 2) do not represent the annual totals, which would be about 80 percent more. Thousands of other interstate workers might be at work during months other than the listed peak.

TABLE I

NUMBER OF PERSONS EMPLOYED IN FARM WORK FOR ANY PERIOD DURING SPECIFIC YEARS, BY STATUS, 1949–1965[1]

YEAR	MIGRATORY (THOUSANDS)	NONMIGRATORY (THOUSANDS)	FOREIGN[2] (THOUSANDS)
1949	422	3,718	113
1952	352	2,628	210
1954	365	2,644	321
1956	427	3,149	460
1957	427	3,535	452
1959	477	3,100	455
1960	409	3,284	335
1961	395	3,094	310
1962	380	3,242	217
1963	386	3,212	209
1964	386	2,984	200
1965	466	2,662	36

[1] From *Domestic Migratory Farm Workers,* United States Department of Agriculture (Agricultural Economic Report 121), 1967.

[2] The large numbers represent *braceros* employed on the Pacific Coast. The reduction in 1965 shows the effect of the legislation restricting their importation.

TABLE II PEAK NUMBER OF

STATE	INTRASTATE AND INTERSTATE MIGRANTS EMPLOYED IN PEAK MONTH	PEAK NUMBER OF INTERSTATE MIGRANTS	MONTH OF PEAK EMPLOYMENT
30 states reporting	270,200	183,200	August
California	53,500	18,900	September
Michigan	42,500	35,100	August
Texas	23,800	2,200	November
New York	19,400	18,200	September
Florida	17,800	11,800	February
Oregon	16,400	13,400	August
Ohio	16,200	15,600	September
Washington	13,000	8,400	September
North Carolina	12,900	6,700	July
New Jersey	12,500	12,400	August
Kansas	10,100	5,800	July
Colorado	9,000	8,400	June
Idaho	8,800	8,200	June
Indiana	8,300	8,300	September
Wisconsin	7,100	6,900	August
Montana	6,200	3,500	July
Pennsylvania	6,200	5,200	September

Note: Figures extracted from *Year of Transition: Seasonal Farm Labor, Report from Secretary of Labor*. Figures were not available for twenty states.

MIGRANT WORKERS, 1965

STATE	INTRASTATE AND INTERSTATE MIGRANTS EMPLOYED IN PEAK MONTH	PEAK NUMBER OF INTERSTATE MIGRANTS	MONTH OF PEAK EMPLOYMENT
Connecticut	5,500	4,500	July
Illinois	5,500	5,500	August and September (same number)
Arizona	4,400	2,500	December
Arkansas	3,600	1,700	May
Louisiana	3,600	2,000	April
Wyoming	3,400	3,100	June
Massachusetts	2,350	2,300	August
Utah	1,800	1,600	August
Missouri	1,400	1,100	October
New Mexico	1,400	200	September
New Hampshire	200	100	July, August, October (same number)
Vermont	150	100	September
Maine	100	50	September

Appendix III—Patterns of Migration: The Three Streams

Interstate migrants in the United States follow a more or less standard flow-pattern—moving northward from a home base in the South, picking those crops which are ripe for harvest along the way and then moving on to other fields, and finally returning to their homes. Occasional variations are due to local conditions of climate, harvest seasons, and the introduction of mechanization.

The Atlantic Coast Stream, alternately called the Eastern Stream, begins to move in April or May. Many workers employed in Florida during the early months of the year—February is the peak season—join the northward trek, along with others who have been recruited specifically for the interstate work and may set out from northern Florida or Georgia. From May to September (and even October and November for the late fall harvests), about fifty thousand migrants (in 1965), about 90 to 95 percent of them southern Negroes, are "following the sun" from Florida, the southern terminus of the Stream.

The dates conform to the crop cycles in the coastal states. The first major demands for seasonal harvest labor occur in South Carolina during late April or early May. From then

170

Travel Patterns of Seasonal Migratory Agricultural Workers

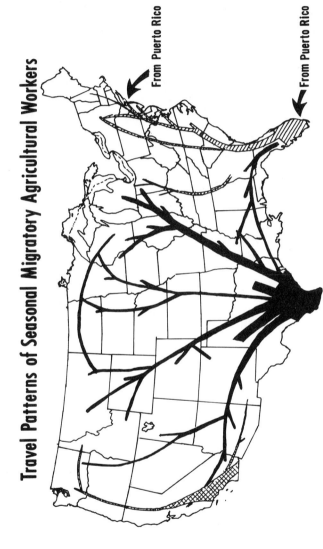

From Puerto Rico

From Puerto Rico

This map shows the major directions of the northward migratory movement of domestic agricultural workers. The movement is reversed as the crop season ends in the northern States and the workers drift back to their home-base areas—for many of them, southern California, Texas, and Florida.

Southern Negroes predominate among the agricultural migrants in the East Coast States and U.S. citizens of Mexican ancestry in the other States. In addition, low-income southern white families, Puerto Ricans, and Indians are found in the domestic agricultural migrant population.

on, the itinerants provide the labor needs at the main producing centers of the various crops. The timing of the labor
needs in the northern states depends upon the harvest
periods of specific crops. In some states north of South
Carolina they are extensive. Beginning in May, the states
of Virginia, Maryland, Delaware, Pennsylvania, New Jersey, and New York need harvesters in ever-increasing numbers. Few workers from the South move into the New
England states, where local labor is adequate. The influx
into the northern states after early June becomes more
rapid until a peak migrant population is reached in late
August or early September.

The harvest needs for specific crops and in different areas
very often overlap. Thus in New York during midseason,
miscellaneous crops—particularly tomatoes, beans, potatoes, peaches, and cherries—are at their peak at the same
time. Similar conditions exist in Virginia, Maryland, New
Jersey, and Pennsylvania, and these states compete with
one another as well as with New York, at identical periods.
These needs for field and orchard labor are, of course,
crucial.

Crews in the Atlantic Coast Stream vary in their schedules of both localities and crops. On the northern trip, some
pass through the South Atlantic states, moving directly into
New Jersey and New York. Others spend most of the season in the Delmarva Peninsula (Delaware, Maryland, and
Virginia) and other sections of the three states. Crews
working first in the north may stop off in other places on
the return trip. These schedules depend on many factors,
particularly the amount of time planned for the entire trip
and whether or not a crew is to work only a special crop like
beans or tomatoes, or pick fruit or ground crops.

The labor is both stoop and upright. The variety of crops

is wide; each requires specialized techniques, some simple and some complicated, for example, when the worker must determine what is ready to pick and what should be left for the next round.

The array of produce and fruits is both varied and plentiful. So pressing are the needs for workers at special times in certain crops that there are often not enough migrants to meet the demand, and Puerto Ricans are being imported increasingly. As yet, harvest mechanization has not been extensive, and human manpower is still in great demand.

The reverse movement, the return south, begins in mid-September, but some workers remain until mid-December harvesting the late and hardy crops.

The Central Stream, alternately called the Middle-West or Midcontinent Stream, is the most complicated and intricate of the three major migrant patterns; it actually consists of several streams. The home base is Texas which, as far as migratory labor is concerned, is like an upturned cornucopia annually pouring forth a human flood of wandering workers. Mexican-Americans (or American Mexicans) make up about 90 percent of the 150,000 total, with a sprinkling of Negroes and southern whites; they are often called Texicans. From Texas, after winter and spring work in vegetables, fruits, and other crops, or in local nonagricultural activities, the workers fan out in four major branches or substreams. Each of these four paths is of comparatively small breadth, perhaps a hundred miles, though work may be found off a main substream in different parts of each state, so that a crew may center its activities in a particular area once it has arrived. The Mexican-Americans tend to work for longer periods in one limited area in which they settle down.

Because of the nineteen states covered by the Central

Stream, the distances covered in the on-the-season travels of these migrants are the longest of the three streams. A round trip may cover up to two or three thousand miles. For this reason, more families take to the road in order to remain together. They also travel less in their own automobiles, finding more security in obtaining both work and shelter by journeying in trucks under the care of crew leaders. More families than single workers are transported in the trucks— trucks are used more than buses—and, in disregard of the federal child labor laws, most of the children over eight years old work in the fields.

The largest army advances up the Mississippi Valley from the Gulf to the Great Lakes, through Arkansas, southeast Missouri, and Illinois, into Indiana, Michigan, and Wisconsin. This movement begins in April and the return trip may not be made until November. A second group starts later, beginning in May or early summer, and moves directly north through Oklahoma, Kansas, Nebraska, and the Dakotas, with an alternate branch going into western Iowa and Minnesota. This stream consists principally of male work crews in wheat and small-grain harvests, and few families follow it. A third major substream moves northwest through the Texas Panhandle and into Colorado and Wyoming. Most of their work is in sugar beets, but this harvest is completed by mid-July, when the fruit and vegetables are ready to be picked. The fourth branch, with its beginning point in western Texas, spreads westward into New Mexico and the abundantly irrigated acreages of southern Arizona, even into southern California, where many workers join the Pacific Coast Stream. A tributary branch moves northward into, first, southern, then northern, Nevada, on into Idaho, and to the Pacific Northwest states of Oregon and Washington. Because of their location at the northern end of the lengthy Pacific Coast Stream, work is abundant in the latter two states, and many of the west Texicans regularly travel the more than fifteen hundred miles involved to reach there.

A look at the map will explain the extensive variations in the crops the interstate migrants harvest. As in the Atlantic Coast Stream, the local climatic conditions are extremely diverse, yet the cycle of harvests permits continuous northward movement, if desired, or extended stays in a specific area. The climate is the chief determinant of the time of the harvest periods. Work is available beginning in early May and continuing as long as the last of November. Because of crop variations, most of the nineteen states have two peak harvest periods, the first from May through July, the second in October and November. During the lull, if workers do not return to their Texas home bases, scattered work is available. Some crews make two annual trips, the first far into the northern states, the second to the nearer states, or vice versa. Those who follow the east branch into the Great Lakes region are assured of continuous work from May until late in the fall months.

The list of the major crops requiring migrant harvesters in the states covered by the four paths of the Central Stream is almost endless. The types of crops in each of the branches are rarely identical, but even so some duplication exists.

Thousands of workers in the Central Stream perform both stoop and upright labor; some work only in the fields, others only in the orchards. Peak seasons are everywhere present. To the Texicans, the annual northward movement is essential in the economic and routine pattern of their lives. The vast products of the soil continue to tempt them from year to year until the six-month trip has become an established, regularly scheduled way of life.

The Pacific Coast (Western) Stream is the most direct and branchless. It is limited to a single strip with variations in breadth, and the out-of-state migrants follow a northward pattern in the central part of the three coastal states—California, Oregon, and Washington. Beginning work in southern Arizona, the Mexican-Americans proceed to southern California, where the band is widest, and work their way up through the center of the three states, veering eastward to harvest the crops of southern Washington, particularly in the Columbia River Basin, where they are often joined by their fellow-Texicans who are arriving at the end of the western branch of the Central Stream. Because of the two crop seasons in California, a large number of workers remain within the state, working up and down in the harvesting of a wide diversity of crops, chiefly vegetables, fruits, and nuts. Their harvest work lasts approximately from May through December.

Many workers in the Pacific Coast Stream start from southern California and either work within the state or progress northward. As pointed out in the text, American citizens have replaced the formerly immense numbers of imported *braceros* in California, and increased use has been made of local and intrastate labor of both the day- and long-haul types.

Nowhere is the pattern of the crop cycle more varied than in California. Because of unique soil and climatic conditions, the state's agricultural production is unequaled both in crop types and extent. The vast variety of soils and the division of seasons into two periods—a short rainy season and a long stretch of warm and sunny days without rainfall—result in continuous harvests, with related labor demands. More than 180 crops are now produced throughout the year, and harvest work is always available in some part of its farmlands. The seasonal pattern followed in the other streams—that of progressive harvests from south to north —does not regularly exist in California, for identical crops may be ripe in different parts of the state at the same time, owing to both the extensive south-north distance and the crop-ripening seasons.

Oregon's dependence on workers from out of the state is less than half that of California. Many of these workers start from west Texas, work in New Mexico and Arizona, and then travel northwest through Utah and Nevada to the harvest in Oregon. Fellow workers in Arizona continue westward toward the Pacific Coast Stream and rarely advance farther than the valleys of central California. While Washington obtains some out-of-state workers from those who have traveled north in the Pacific Coast Stream, it also receives a considerable number who pass through eastern Oregon into Washington at the north end of the Central Stream. The state is therefore the northern terminus for two migrant flows.

The heaviest demands for seasonal work in Oregon are in the northern part of the state, where the major crops are ready to harvest from June to November. The pattern is more localized, with peak periods in June and August. Washington, particularly in the southern areas, has very much the same crops as Oregon. For example, the peach season overlaps in western Oregon from August 10 to September 18 and in northern Washington from August 7 to August 31. Cherries are an example of the south-to-north harvest cycle: they ripen in northern Oregon from June 8 to July 10, and in eastern Washington during the entire month of July. The Washington peak labor periods are similar to those of Oregon, forming a somewhat competitive labor market.

Sources and Readings

This list is highly selective. Magazine articles may be located in *Readers' Guide* under the headings "Migrant labor" and "Children of migrant laborers." United States government publications are listed in the *Monthly Catalog* under "Farm labor" and "Migrant labor."

United States government publications and documents, which contain much valuable material on the migrant laborer, are often difficult to obtain. Those included here date for the most part from the major legislation enacted in 1962 and 1963; those of earlier date are landmark documents, now out of print. The symbol † indicates that the item is for sale by the Superintendent of Documents, Government Printing Office, Washington, D.C. 20402; the GPO number indicated should be used when ordering. Those with the symbol * are available in depository libraries, or may be obtained from the issuing agency or office when a code number is included. Congressional hearings and Committee Prints have limited printings and distribution, and are available only in depository libraries.

General Works

ALLEN, STEVE. *The Ground Is Our Table*. Doubleday, 1966.

†*Farm Labor Fact Book*. United States Department of Labor, 1959, pp. 82–146, 214–226. GPO: L 1.2:F22.

HARRINGTON, MICHAEL. *The Other America: Poverty in the United States*. Macmillan, 1962, pp. 39–60. Paperback, Penguin Special S223, pp. 43–62.

HILL, HERBERT. *No Harvest for the Reaper*. National Association for the Advancement of Colored People, 1960.

KOCH, WILLIAM H., JR. *Dignity of Their Own*. Friendship Press, 1966.

——. *Next Move for the Migrants*. Friendship Press, 1966.

MOORE, TRUMAN E. *The Slaves We Rent*. Random House, 1965.

SHOTWELL, LOUISA R. *The Harvesters: The Story of the Migrant People*. Doubleday, 1961.

——. *Roosevelt Grady*. World, 1963. Paperback, Grosset & Dunlap, Tempo No. 4767.

——. *This Is the Migrant*. Friendship Press, 1968.

WRIGHT, DALE. *They Harvest Despair: The Migrant Farm Worker*. Beacon Press, 1965.

Chapter 1—Our American Migrant Farm Workers

MCWILLIAMS, CAREY. *Factories in the Field: The Story of Migratory Farm Labor in California*. Little, Brown, 1939.

——. *Ill Fares the Land: Migrants and Migratory Labor in the United States*. Little, Brown, 1942. Reprint, Barnes & Noble, 1967.

STEINBECK, JOHN. *The Grapes of Wrath*. Viking Press, 1939. Many editions. Paperback, Bantam No. N2710.

*United States Department of Labor. Labor Standards Bureau. *Report to the President on Domestic Migratory Farm Labor* (President's Committee on Migratory Labor). 1961. Code: L 16.43/R29/960.

*United States President's Commission on Migratory Labor. *Migratory Labor in American Agriculture*. 1951. Out of print.

*United States Public Health Service. *Domestic Agricultural Migrants in the United States: Counties in Which an Estimated 100 or More Seasonal Workers Migrated into the Area to Work During the Peak Season*. 1965 (Publication 540). Code: FS 2.2:M/58/2/966. Also in United States Senate Committee on Labor and Welfare, Subcommittee on Migratory Labor, *1968 Report,* pp. 69–89.

*United States Senate. Committee on Labor and Public Welfare. Subcommittee on Migratory Labor. 86th Congress, 2d Session. *The Migrant Farm Worker in America: Background Data on the Migrant Worker Situation in the United States Today,* by DANIEL H. POLLITT and SELMA M. LEVINE. 1960. Committee Print.

History of Agricultural Migrations

FOSTER, PHILLIPS. "Migrations and Agriculture," United States Department of Agriculture, *Yearbook of Agriculture, 1964,* pp. 22–29.

The Rural-to-Urban Movement

"How U.S. Is Changing: People on the Move," *U. S. News & World Report,* Vol. 59 (November 15, 1965), pp. 74–78.

Movement of Negroes to Cities

BONTEMPS, ARNA, and CONROY, JACK. *Anyplace But Here.* Hill & Wang, 1966.

NEWMAN, DOROTHY K. "The Negro's Journey to the City," *Monthly Labor Review,* Vol. 88 (May and June 1965), pp. 502–507, 644–650.

Selected State Studies

California. Senate. Fact Finding Committee on Labor and Welfare. *California's Farm Labor Problems* (Cobey Report). 2 vols., 1963.

Colorado. Legislative Council. *Migratory Labor in Colorado: Report to the General Assembly.* 1962. (Research Publication 72).

Florida. Legislative Council and Legislative Reference Bureau. *Migrant Farm Labor in Florida.* 1963.

Maryland. Governor's Committee on Migratory Labor. *Progress in Meeting Problems of Migratory Labor in Maryland, 1963–1966: Report.* 1967.

Oregon. Bureau of Labor. . . . *And Migrant Problems Demand Attention.* 1959.

Chapter 5—Getting the Work

†United States Department of Agriculture. Economic Research Service. *Seasonal Work Patterns of the Hired Working Force for 1964,* and *1965 Supplement* (Agricultural Economic Report 102). 1966, 1967. GPO: A 93.28.-102.

*United States Department of Labor. Employment Security Bureau. *Major Agricultural Migrant Labor Demand Areas (by Month and Principal Crops).* Annual.

*———. Farm Labor Service. *Guides to Seasonal Farm Work Areas:* Eastern Seaboard States, Gulf to the Great Lakes, Intermountain States, Far Western States. 4 maps. Annual. Code: L.7.25/3:F22/3.

*———. Farm Labor Service. *Peak Seasonal Farm Labor Force and Crop Production Centers.* Wall Map and Guide. Annual.

Chapter 6—Key Man: The Crew Leader

*United States Department of Labor. Employment Security Bureau. *Information About Registration of Interstate Farm Labor Contractors.* 1966. Code: L 7.2:F22/13.

*———. Labor Standards Bureau. *Major Provisions of State and Federal Farm Labor Contractor Laws.* 1965 (Bulletin 275). Code L 16.3:275.

*United States Interstate Commerce Commission. *To Crew Leaders, Drivers, and Owners of Vehicles Transporting Migratory Farm Workers.* 1963. Code: IC 1.12/2:-M58.

Chapter 7—Profile of the Interstate Migrant

Koos, Earl. *They Follow the Sun.* Jacksonville: Florida State Board of Health, 1957 (Monograph No. 1), pp. 12–54.

†United States Department of Agriculture. Economic Research Service. *Domestic Migratory Farm Workers: Personal and Economic Characteristics.* 1967 (Agricultural Economic Report 121). GPO: A 93.28:121.

Unionization and Collective Bargaining

Allen, Steve. *The Ground Is Our Table.* Doubleday, 1966, pp. 105–127.

Dunne, John G. *Delano: The Story of the California Grape Strike.* Farrar, Straus & Giroux, 1967.

———. "Strike! California Grape Pickers," *Saturday Evening Post,* Vol. 240 (May 6, 1967), pp. 32–36.

Farm Labor Organizing, 1905–1967: A Brief History. New York: National Advisory Committee on Farm Labor, 1967.

"March of the Migrants," *Life,* Vol. 60 (April 29, 1966), pp. 93–94.

Chapter 8—The Home Away from Home

Hogarty, Richard A. *New Jersey Farmers and Migrant Housing Rules.* Bobbs-Merrill, 1966 (Inter-University Case Program 94).

†United States Department of Agriculture. *Housing for Seasonal Farm Workers: Designs and Design Suggestions.* 1965

(Agriculture Information Bulletin 296). GPO: A 1.65:296.

†————, and United States Public Health Service. *Family Housing for Migrant Agricultural Workers.* 1967. GPO: A 77.6/3:H81.

*United States Department of Labor. Employment Security Bureau. *Housing Handbook: A Guide to Improved Farm Worker Housing.* 1967. Code: L 7.25/3/H81.

*————. Manpower Administration. *Housing Regulations of the United States Department of Labor for Out-of-State Agricultural . . . Workers Recruited Through State Employment Service.* 1967. Code: L 7.25:H81.

Chapter 9—The Welfare of the Workers

*United States Department of Labor. Labor Standards Bureau. *Coverage of Agricultural Workers Under State and Federal Labor Laws.* 1964 (Bulletin 264). Code: L 16.3:264.

*————. *Status of Agricultural Workers Under State and Federal Labor Laws.* (Fact Sheet 2, December 1965). Code: L 16.50.2 (rev.)

Health

BROWNING, R. H. and NORTHCUTT, T. J., JR. *On the Season: A Report of a Public Health Project Conducted Among Negro Migrant Agricultural Workers in Palm Beach County, Florida.* Jacksonville: Florida State Board of Health. 1961 (Monograph No. 2), pp. 29–61.

*United States Public Health Service. *Grants for Migrant Family Health Services* (Under Migrant Health Act of 1962). 1965 (Publication 971). Code: FS 2.2:-M58/4/965.

*United States Senate. Committee on Labor and Public Welfare. 88th Congress, 1st Session. *Adequate Sanitation Facilities for Migratory Farm Laborers, Report to Accompany S. 526.* 1963. Senate Report 199.

*———. Subcommittee on Migratory Labor. 90th Congress, 1st Session. *Migrant Health Program: Current Operations and Additional Needs.* 1967. Committee Print.

*———. Subcommittee on Migratory Labor. 90th Congress, 1st Session. *Migrant Health Services: Hearings on S. 2688 to Amend the Health Services Act.* 1967. Committee Print.

Community Relations

HARPER, THELMA H. *Project CASE: Community Action with the Seasonally Employed.* Washington, National Consumers Committee for Research and Education, 1966.

†United States Department of Labor. Labor Standards Bureau. *The Community Meets the Migrant Worker: Current Programs and Trends.* 1960 (Bulletin 221). GPO: L 16.3:221.

*———. *State Committees on Seasonal Agricultural Labor: Their Organization and Programs.* 1965 (Bulletin 274). Code: L 16.3:274.

*———. *Welcome Stranger! A Guide to Community Efforts to Improve Conditions for Agricultural Migrants.* 1964 (Bulletin 258). Code: L 16.3:258 (rev.).

Chapter 10—The Plight of the Children

Health and Day Care

SIEGEL, EARL. "Health and Day Care for Children of Migrant Workers," *Public Health Reports,* Vol. 79 (October 1964), pp. 847–852.

*United States Senate. Committee on Labor and Public Welfare. 88th Congress, 1st Session. *Day-Care Services for Migrant Farm Children, Report to Accompany S. 522.* 1963. Senate Report 198.

Education

HANEY, GEORGE F. "Problems and Trends in Migrant Education," *School Life,* Vol. 45 (July 1963), pp. 5–9.

†———. *Selected State Programs in Migrant Education.* United States Office of Education *Bulletin,* 1963, No. 45. GPO: FS 5.223:23030.

McGehee, Florence. *Please Excuse Johnny.* Macmillan, 1952.

Sadler, Ann. "Mees, You Goin' to be Real Teacher Now, Don'cha?" *American Education,* Vol. 3 (May 1967), pp. 14–16. Same abridged, "Worst Bunch in School." *Reader's Digest,* Vol. 91 (July 1967), pp. 182–184, 186, 188.

Sharp, Emmit F. and Larson, Olaf F. *Migratory Farm Workers in the Atlantic Coast Stream II. Education of New York Workers and Their Children, 1953 and 1957.* Ithaca: New York State College of Agriculture, 1960 (Bulletin 949).

*United States Senate. Committee on Labor and Public Welfare. 88th Congress, 1st Session. *Improved Educational Opportunities for Migratory Workers and Their Children, Report to Accompany S. 524.* 1963. Senate Report 201.

Chapter 11—Man Versus Machine

An abundant number of articles on the harvesting of various crops may be located in the *Biological and Agricultural Index* and *Readers' Guide* under the heading "Harvesting machinery."

Boykin, John E. "Weird New World of Old MacDonald," *Popular Mechanics,* Vol. 126 (July 1966), pp. 112–115.

"Harvest Machines Seek Wider Fields: Devices That Can Select as Well as Pick," *Business Week,* December 3, 1966, pp. 164–166.

Kelly, C. F. "Mechanical Harvesting." *Scientific American,* Vol. 217 (August 1967), pp. 50–59.

McBride, John G. *Vanishing Bracero.* San Antonio: Naylor, 1963.

Chapter 12—A Fair Deal

†President's National Advisory Commission on Rural Poverty. *The People Left Behind; Report.* 1967. GPO: Pr 36.8:R88/P39.

United States Senate. Committee on Labor and Public Welfare. Subcommittee on Migratory Labor. *The Migratory Farm Labor Problem in the United States. Reports.*
1964, 88th Congress, 2d Session. Senate Report 934.
1965, 89th Congress, 1st Session. Senate Report 155.
1966, 89th Congress, 2nd Session. Senate Report 1549.
1967, 90th Congress, 1st Session. Senate Report 71.
1968, 90th Congress, 2nd Session. Senate Report 1006.

These form the best summary of work on current federal legislation.

Appendix III—Patterns of Migration

Atlantic Coast Stream

BROWNING, R. H., and NORTHCUTT, T. J., JR. *On the Season.* Jacksonville: Florida State Board of Health, 1961 (Monograph No. 2), pp. 5–14.

KOOS, EARL L. *They Follow the Sun.* Jacksonville: Florida State Board of Health, 1957 (Monograph No. 1), pp. 2–7.

LARSON, OLAF F., and SHARP, EMMIT F. *Migratory Farm Workers in the Atlantic Coast Stream: I. Changes in New York, 1955 and 1957.* Ithaca, New York: State College of Agriculture, 1960 (Bulletin 948).

McWILLIAMS, CAREY. *Ill Fares the Land.* Little, Brown, 1942; reprint, Barnes & Noble, 1967, pp. 168–185.

*United States Department of Agriculture. *Migratory Farm Workers in the Atlantic Coast Stream . . . ,* by WILLIAM

H. METZLER. 1955 (Circular 966). Code: A 1.4/2:-966.

The Central Stream

McWILLIAMS, CAREY. *Ill Fares the Land.* Little, Brown, 1942; reprint, Barnes & Noble, 1967. pp. 71–146, 257–281.
*United States Department of Agriculture. *Migratory Farm Workers in the Midcontinent Streams,* by WILLIAM H. METZLER, and F. O. SARGENT. 1960. Code: A 1.84:-41.

The Pacific Coast Stream

Bracero Program

LEARY, MARY E. "As the Braceros Leave," *Reporter,* Vol. 32 (January 28, 1965), pp. 43–45.
†United States Department of Agriculture. Economic Research Service. *Termination of the Bracero Program, Some Effects on Farm Labor and Migrant Housing Needs,* by ROBERT MCELROY and EARL C. GARETT. 1965 (Agricultural Economic Report 77). GPO: A 93.28:77.
"When U.S. Barred Foreign Workers from Farms: Bracero Ban," *U. S. News & World Report,* Vol. 58 (May 31, 1965), pp. 73–75.

Index

Page numbers for principal treatments are indicated in italics